creating MONSTERS

FINDING FAME IN JESUS' NAME

KEITH STANCIL

Artist Garden Publishing

Nashville

© 2015 by Keith Stancil

All rights reserved. No portion of this book may be reproduced, stored in a retrieval system, or transmitted in any form or by any means—electronic, mechanical, photocopy, recording, scanning, or other—except for brief quotations in critical reviews or articles, without the prior written permission of the publisher.

Published in Nashville, Tennessee by Artist Garden Publishing

Edited by Lindsay Williams
Cover Design by Keith Stancil / Sarah Siegand
Interior Design by Sarah Siegand

All Scripture quotations, unless otherwise notated, are taken from the ESV Bible (The Holy Bible, English Standard Version) copyright © 2001 by Crossway, a publishing ministry of Good News Publishers. Used by permission. All rights reserved.

Scripture quotations from THE MESSAGE. Copyright © by Eugene H. Peterson 1993, 1994, 1995, 1996, 2000, 2001, 2002. Used by permission of Tyndale House Publishers, Inc.

This book is dedicated to my sweet wife, Diana.
The most beautiful woman inside and out with a heart full of love for all.

acknowledgments

Jesus - Thanks for your overwhelming love and grace.

Diana - Thanks for teaching me how to show love to all, for encouraging me to follow the dreams God put in my heart and for your unwavering support in all I do.

Dad & Mom - Thank you for bringing me into the world and for your intentional efforts to raise me in a Godly environment. Your persistent prayers and teaching helped build the foundation I stand on today.

Julian & Elizabeth, Dion, Jaci & Nic - Thanks for welcoming me into your family late in life. You each inspire me in unique ways.

Zealand, Soren, Isabella - Thank you for the joy you bring to my life. Your innocent love and desire to learn give me hope for the future.

Kate - I'm so grateful for the benefits I receive in Diana because of the love you poured into her throughout her life. Your unwavering dedication to God is an encouraging example to our family.

Michael Easley, Llyod Shadrach, Jeff Shulte, Bill Wellons, Stephen Mansfield, Jerry Sutton, Dean Haun, Bill Hightower, Randy Kennedy - Thank you for the biblical teaching throughout my life. God has used you in mighty ways to lead me to a deeper understanding of His truth.

Tom Clagett - Thank you for challenging me to dive deeper into the Word and for being intentional in gathering men to study the Bible together.

Larry & Anne Kayser - You are the true model of a pastor and teacher. Thanks for pouring your wisdom into Diana & I with all your heart.

Dave Buehring - Thanks for serving as my pastor, teacher, mentor and friend. You have challenged me to go deeper with God through listening to Him. Your encouragement provided the kick start for stepping out on faith and doing something with the vision God gave me.

Roland Lundy, Mark Funderburg, Terry London - Thank you for showing me what it looks like to operate on an executive business level while maintaining integrity and allowing God to navigate. I will be forever grateful for the opportunity I had to serve under your leadership.

Kevin Hyer - God blessed me when he put you in my life. Thank you for your encouragement, accountability, prayers and, most of all, your friendship.

David Chaudhry - You have been an incredible asset to my life. I admire your tenacity in loving Jesus and walking with excellence in every step you take in life. Thanks for your friendship and for setting an incredible example for others of what it looks like to walk with and honor God.

Pete Orta - Thanks for your friendship, encouragement and for showing me what it looks like to step out in total faith. The impact you are having on young men's lives is an incredible example for all.

Gabe, Holly, Ryan, Noah, Tal, David and Licia - I'm grateful to have the opportunity to walk alongside you daily in ministry. Thanks for following the call and for sustaining an unwavering faith.

Lindsay Williams - Thanks for polishing up my hillbilly writing and helping me express my thoughts clearly.

contents

    Foreword 13

    Preface 17

1. Opening Scene 19
2. The Birth of Dr. Frankenstein 25
3. Monster Academy 33
4. Little Monsters 39
5. The Monster Ego 45
6. Monsters of Entitlement 53
7. Monsters of More 59
8. Monsters in the Closet 63
9. Monsters of Rock 67
10. Parental Monsters 75
11. Monsters of Worship 81
12. Platform vs. Stage 89
13. Social Network Monsters 95
14. The Abominable Snowman 101
15. Monsters of Finance 109
16. Monsters of Commitment 115
17. Monster Music 121
18. Killing the Monster 125
19. Turn on the Lights 129

    My Prayer 133

FOREWORD

BY DAVID BUEHRING

Aren't artists amazing? They are some of the most wonderful, gifted, God-graced and fun people that I have the privilege of walking alongside. I enjoy their company, creativity, spontaneity and ability to fully engage in the moment. Their depth of insight, unique vantage point and originality with words and/or sounds can often marvelously reflect the greatness and glory of their Maker. What an absolute gift they are from Jesus to this world!

I've had the privilege of relating to many artists as a pastor, discipler, guide and friend for well over three decades. I like asking them, "Are you first an artist or a disciple of Jesus?" Of course, I know they are both, but their answer helps me understand *who* will define them, *who* they will reflect, and *who* will influence the decisions they make regarding their lives and callings. Although most begin with the answer "a disciple of Jesus," I've found that over time, attitudes, decisions, and actions often default to a harmonizing with what's trending rather than a heartbeat for extending Jesus throughout His Church and around the world.

With the name of Jesus, the essential mission of His Kingdom, and a lost and dying planet at stake, it's time for the creative community of God to rise to what may be its greatest "for such a time as this" moment! To get there, however, will require some realignment to the character and ways of God, revealed in the Scriptures. It will mean that artists, musicians, songwriters, producers, promoters, executives, and managers need to yield their agendas to His Plan. It necessitates that "career building" be reoriented to "disciple-making"; that "stages to perform" return to "platforms of service"; and that the subtle and deceptive desire to be idolized is fully crucified so that it can be resurrected with passion and power to see Jesus glorified!

So, how do we get from "here" to "there"? Has a thought-trail been blazed for us to consider? Are there godly principles that we can obey and reference along the way? If so, who has taken the time to pave a way for us to walk in?

This is where my friend, Keith Stancil, comes in.

As a veteran of the music industry, including the last two decades spent interacting with hundreds of artists who are followers of Jesus, Keith has penned a reference guide for us that can aid in realignment. *Creating Monsters* has been laid out in nineteen reflective devotional-sized chapters where Keith shares the heart of God in practical ways. Each chapter is loaded with insights from his experiences with the music world and his own journey with God. Although he'd be the first to say he's not an expert on the topic; he is, in fact, a wise, godly voice that needs to be heard by all who make arts and entertainment their primary realm of service. His observations are spot on, his solutions both scriptural and doable…especially if one's heart loves Jesus so much that their greatest desire is to walk in obedience to Him.

I believe that many of the godly men and women whom I've walked with in the world of music will echo a hearty "hear, hear" after a read of *Creating Monsters*. I look forward to getting my hands on dozens of copies to personally hand out to my friends who serve at every level and in every genre! I can see music executives and managers using this tool to get their artists more in tune with the ways of God. I imagine tour buses becoming mobile small groups applying the content while on the road. And, I can see seasoned artists discipling emerging artists to make sure their foundations are godly, healthy, Kingdom-oriented, and God honoring.

I highly commend both Keith and *Creating Monsters* to you. Read it. Reflect on the truths presented. Where needed, repent and realign–or rejoice and reengage! And after you've allowed it to penetrate your own soul, consider whom it is around you that may need the same touch from God, and pass it on to them. I'd encourage you to even go a step further by leading a group of your peers through it.

We are living in a time in history where much is on the line around the world. We have an incredible opportunity to see Jesus move even more powerfully through those He's uniquely designed with creative gifts to aid in the reviving of His Church, to see more of the lost found and the nations transformed. The people who make up the creative community of God are part of God's "front lines"–arrows that can be strategically fired by the Lord to free captives from demonic strongholds and minister to hurting souls via their miracle-empowered melodies, while rousing warriors to rise up to obey the call of God on their lives! It's time–let's do this!

– DAVE BUEHRING
Lionshare Founder & President
Author of *A Discipleship Journey* and *The Jesus Blueprint*
www.davebuehring.com
Franklin, Tennessee

PREFACE

The monster lurks within pretending to be one with our human soul. It hides in the shadows hoping to go unnoticed until the opportune time to launch its attack. Posing as the answer to the perfect life, the monster lures us in to feed it. Our decision "to feed" or "not to feed" determines the fate or survival of the monster.

Working in the entertainment industry has given me a front row seat to witness the monster's cunning work. Struggling with the monster in my own life has given me a keen sense of its presence and its ability to quickly move into a position of control over one's life. God has placed a strong desire in my heart to equip others with the ability to recognize early signs of the monster and to point them toward the resistance resource only He provides.

God places some on large platforms for the purpose of making Jesus famous. Artists, musicians, actors, professional athletes, authors, speakers and corporate ladder climbers can easily lose sight of God's intended purpose for their lives. My hope is that this book will bring an awareness of the monster's presence and equip those pursuing careers on platforms with the necessary tools to navigate potential fame with biblical excellence.

Everyone to whom much was given, of him much will be required.
(Luke 12:48, ESV)

chapter one:
OPENING SCENE

Winding through the Tennessee hills, I found myself lost in dreamy conversation. Similar drives over the years have served as the perfect backdrop for birthing new ideas, and this particular drive was no exception. The drive was bursting with excitement over new frontiers my wife, Diana, and I were embarking on. Our recent launch of an artist management company filled a desire that had been brewing in my soul for years. As we made our way over Monteagle and descended toward Nickajack Lake and the Tennessee/Georgia border, I dreamed while Diana mostly listened. Diana had previously visited this unchartered territory of artist management that I was so eager to explore. Her wisdom-filled experience was full of caution, but her love for me transcended any reservations, causing her to nurture the desires of my heart. Diana silenced any hesitancy she may have been feeling and trusted that God had planted that desire in me for a purpose. And so the great adventure began.

An invitation to see a new artist perform at a youth event was the catalyst for this day trip. Driving up to the venue, my curiosity for what this young band would sound like was elevated. As a new management company, we were eager to find the "next big artist." The band had grabbed our attention through some recent media coverage, but their online performances weren't really enough to make an accurate analysis. The band members were cute and photogenic, but did they have what it takes to launch a substantial career in music? Unfortunately, the show was disappointing. With an audience of maybe twenty people, it was obvious the band was still learning how to master their instruments and would need quite a bit of help with stage presence and songwriting. After the show, I wanted so badly to pull an Elvis exit by jumping in the car and driving away before anyone noticed we were gone. Even though running would have been much easier, Diana talked me into saying a few words before we left. She often compares me to "American Idol's" Simon Cowell due to my brutal honesty. Diana, on the other hand, has an incredibly compassionate heart and pleaded with me to be nice and talk to the young band before leaving.

Somehow, we were talked into managing the band and set out on the arduous journey of developing their talent. Developing the young band proved to be a terribly painstaking process. Not because they were so far off as musicians, but because they argued with us every step of the way. The band members were convinced they knew everything about the music business and challenged most of the advice we offered. While I'm not normally one for waving my own accomplishment flag, I had to remind the band often of the fourteen million records I personally sold during my twenty-five-year career.

In addition to the argumentative band members, there were pushy parents involved, which made our task even more difficult. From day one, I spent hours listening to the parents of each of the band members complain about why the music industry would be overlooking their children who were already incredible stars in the parents' minds. The parents would relentlessly argue against most advice we offered, which made our journey miserable at times.

Moreover, another group that was also pursuing a music career appeared in a high-profile battle of the bands contest with the young band and created an unhealthy competitiveness in the minds of the band members and their parents. Many of our conversations were laced with their envy toward what was going on with the other band. I would regularly remind them how the Bible instructs us to not allow envy to enter our hearts.

> *If we live by the Spirit, let us also keep in step with the Spirit. Let us not become conceited, provoking one another, envying one another.*
> (Galatians 5:25-26, ESV)

The young musicians and their parents had, somewhere along the way, confused striving for excellence with a dangerous amount of jealousy. They masked envy under the guise of healthy competitiveness. Unfortunately, mis-managed jealousy eats at one's soul, creating an insatiable appetite for more and making it impossible to find peace. Jealousy is labeled as unspiritual and demonic in the Bible.

> *But if you have bitter jealousy and selfish ambition in your hearts, do not boast and be false to the truth. This is not the wisdom that comes down from above, but is earthly, unspiritual, demonic. For where jealousy and selfish ambition exist, there will be disorder and every vile practice.*
> (James 3:14-16, ESV)

The inability to find peace and contentment has robbed personal joy from countless musicians, so we continued the task of helping them learn to abate their jealousy. Even though their arguing and jealousy caused disorder and became extremely tiresome, I continued pushing through to complete the task.

Never desiring to work with rock stars, I attempted to mentor the young band in a way that would hopefully prevent them from becoming another casualty of fame. I certainly didn't want to help turn them into "Disney kid stars" who would one day regret chasing someone else's dream, so we spent hours with the band talking through the direction they desired to take. Their parents were pushing them toward chasing mainstream success, but we wanted to know the band members' hearts. Diana and I spent time praying that God would use us to help tame any monsters that might be lurking within the hearts of the band members. After much soul searching, the band determined that they wanted to be a Christian band. While that was music to my ears, only time would tell if their desire and calling to do Christian music was genuine or if they really wanted to be rock stars.

chapter two:
THE BIRTH OF DR. FRANKENSTEIN

At the age of eight, I had a church experience which I thought, at the time, was becoming a Christian. I walked the aisle, said a few words to the preacher and followed in baptism. It was an extremely scary experience for a child to go through because so much emphasis was put on the act of public display. I remember feeling different but not totally understanding why. Thinking I still needed to earn my way into heaven, I began trying to live by a set of legalistic rules taught to me at the Southern Baptist church our family attended. Around the age of twelve, I graduated into the youth group still a bit unsure of the journey I was on. Our youth group had some amazing times singing "Pass It On" and getting emotionally pumped about Jesus. Even though I was blessed with loving, diligent teachers, I somehow missed connecting the simple dots of the Gospel. The sinner's prayer was prayed but experiencing God was absent, and I soon ended up chasing other things in life. Looking back, I now see the Holy Spirit was calling me to Jesus during that time. Thankfully, Jesus offers unending grace, as I would take a few wrong turns before eventually finding my way back to Him.

creating MONSTERS

Fascinated by the underlying rhythm of music, a deep desire in my soul to play the drums quickly became an obsession. The relentless practice of banging on things soon blossomed into praise from others for my newly developed skills. Little did I know, my future bandmates were on the other side of town honing similar musical skills. And then it happened...my first jam session!

I remember my first jam session from thirty-five years ago in Snellville, Georgia, like it were yesterday. My friends and I played a version of the Doobie Brothers' "China Grove" for three solid hours. Playing music with other musicians was an exhilarating feeling and one I would immediately become addicted to. My new found freedom in music took me places I never imagined. Eventually, we invited friends over to listen. Performing renditions of Lynyrd Skynyrd's "Sweet Home Alabama" and "Free Bird" catapulted us to rock star status amongst friends in our small Georgia town. The adoration and worship our friends poured on us felt wonderful and gave me a small taste of what it must be like for a celebrity rock star. I also quickly learned how playing rock 'n' roll and wearing spandex pants drew a great deal of attention from females, which is often the primary goal for teenage boys. As my rock star skills developed, so did the desire to be worshipped. The once innocent little church boy found himself playing Atlanta clubs in pursuit of the rock star dream.

After graduating from college, my short-lived dream of stardom hit a dead end and I found myself working for Capitol Records, helping others become rock stars. The kind folks at Capitol taught me how to build and feed egos. Of course, we would then complain when the artists found success and their egos grew out of control. My newly-found music business job actually turned out to be a career in the ego-building business.

I remember working a concert with one of our top rock acts where I was asked to go find a few beautiful girls for the band and give them backstage passes. What an exhilarating task for a record company newbie! Feeling

THE BIRTH OF DR. FRANKENSTEIN

powerful as the backstage pass distributor, my own ego was boosted into overdrive. Soon the world would know how cool I was! However, what I witnessed backstage at that show was extremely unsettling as I saw how easily those young girls offered themselves to the rock stars. My glorious job of backstage pass distributing was nothing more than serving as a groupie pimp for the band. Fortunately, God used that haunting experience as a pivotal moment in my career by creating a stirring in my heart and causing me to question what I was contributing to the world.

My record label career continued on for eight years with Capitol and eventually Warner Brothers. The job became my identity, creating a very shallow life. While I made a number of life-long friends, which I am thankful for, building egos proved to be very unrewarding. Soon, the decadence and extravagance of the music industry began to implode, causing music sales to decline. The inevitable layoffs hit the record companies, and I drew the lucky pink slip finding myself on the street with no job, no identity and extreme emptiness.

With a perfectly orchestrated plan, God used a period of unemployment to alter my life forever. He met me at an extremely low point and ushered in the most beautiful "come to Jesus" experience. I remember crying out to God from a very dark and empty place on the day I lost my job. Feeling abandoned by the world, the memories of my childhood church experience reminded me there is a place to turn. Jesus met me instantly in all His glory. My loving dad and mother had been praying and waiting patiently for this moment for years. Jesus used them in a tremendous way as I began to learn to walk in His grace. I am forever grateful to have been blessed with those parental spiritual rocks and a God who loves me dearly.

As I embarked on my new Christian journey, I felt God calling me to work in Christian music. Word Records, one of the top Christian record labels, had an opening perfectly fit to my skill set. After a long six months of unemployment, Word hired me to help them grow Christian music sales in the mainstream market. Being a true Jesus follower, I was on fire to spread the Gospel message to the nations. I couldn't have imagined a more perfect job. The position allowed me to work with some amazing Christians, including Word's legendary president, Roland Lundy. Much to my surprise, my perception of the Christian music industry would quickly darken as I encountered others who lived lives no different than many in mainstream music. Those dark, unexpected areas protracted significantly as I began to navigate through the industry. I discovered that amongst some of the God-loving people and Christian music moniker were some very lost souls.

During my first week on the job at Word, I found myself in a meeting, listening to a more God-less rant than I had ever experienced on the mainstream side of the business. I remember talking to God that evening and asking Him for forgiveness for taking the job and missing His lead. This new Christian record company job was supposed to be like going to church, right? As I was contemplating quitting, God quickly confirmed I was exactly where He wanted me to be, and my role was to shed a little light amongst any darkness I encountered. Knowing I certainly wasn't perfect myself, I somehow mustered the strength to accept the challenge. Fortunately, along the way, I encountered others at Word and throughout the Christian music industry who were genuinely working toward building God's Kingdom. Throughout the years that followed, God would provide incredible opportunities for us to work together for His purposes.

As I ventured deeper into the Christian music industry role God placed me in, I realized how He was preparing me from day one at Capitol for the position I'm serving in now as an artist manager. The best way to learn how to manage egos is to build them. As a Christian, I would never have chosen a job based on building egos, but I now see how God used my mainstream record label experience to prepare me for the present. God is such an amazing orchestrator.

Even though I have a calling to help manage egos, the biggest task is to first manage my own ego. Jealousy, envy and greed are fuel for the ego and unfortunately, the fall of Adam and Eve filled the entire human race with a copious supply of fuel reserves. Our human need to feel self-important and to be worshipped is definitely not of God. He reiterates that throughout the Bible starting with one of His commandments in Exodus.

And God spoke all these words, saying, "I am the Lord your God, who brought you out of the land of Egypt, out of the house of slavery. "You shall have no other gods before me. "You shall not make for yourself a carved image, or any likeness of anything that is in heaven above, or that is in the earth beneath, or that is in the water under the earth. You shall not bow down to them or serve them, for I the Lord your God am a jealous God, visiting the iniquity of the fathers on the children to the third and the fourth generation of those who hate me, but showing steadfast love to thousands of those who love me and keep my commandments.
(Exodus 20:1-6, ESV)

God's commandment to not bow down and worship anything other than God includes worshipping ourselves. Unfortunately, the desire to be worshipped drives the entertainment business, including some in Christian music. Shouldn't Christians feel convicted when the desire to be worshipped creeps in? If I were an artist seeking to follow Jesus, I would certainly surround myself with accountability in that area. Thankfully, I have a Godly wife who keeps me in check. God uses her (and the Holy Spirit) to let me know when pride and ego are raising their ugly heads.

So how do I avoid becoming Dr. Frankenstein? My calling is to help artists build platforms for ministry, not create monsters. I'm forced to wrestle with that tension daily. God never promised life on earth would be easy, so I must rest in His assurance that He will use me for His glory while I diligently stay focused on Him and His Word. As difficult as it is for my own ego, I have resolved it's okay when my management style doesn't line up with every artist I encounter. Some will fit well within our management relationship, while others will choose to follow their ego. I can only pray God uses me to plant seeds with all artists we have the opportunity to work with, knowing what He does with them from there is in His hands and out of my control.

chapter three:
MONSTER ACADEMY

If you ask most children these days who they want to be when they grow up, they will pick a celebrity. Peyton Manning, Lebron James, Justin Bieber, Taylor Swift, Rihanna, the President of the United States, the Kardashians and David Beckham currently top the list. Similarly, if you ask a young Christian musician who they would like to be, they might say Newsboys, Lecrae, Britt Nicole, Jamie Grace, Switchfoot, Chris Tomlin or Skillet. Why? Because many want to be adored and worshipped by others. They view being a celebrity as a glorious life. Play a little music or professional sports, receive adoration and worship from the masses, make tons of money, live in a big house, drive expensive cars and life is good! There's only one problem. God didn't design us to be worshipped. He instructs us on how we are to live our lives in Philippians 2.

> *Do nothing from selfish ambition or conceit, but in humility count others more significant than yourselves. Let each of you look not only to his own interests, but also to the interests of others. Have this mind*

among yourselves, which is yours in Christ Jesus, who, though he was in the form of God, did not count equality with God a thing to be grasped, but emptied himself, by taking the form of a servant, being born in the likeness of men. And being found in human form, he humbled himself by becoming obedient to the point of death, even death on a cross.
(Philippians 2:3-8, ESV)

Looking closely at those instructions, it appears God wants us humans to remain humble. So much so He sent His son Jesus to earth to give us a model of what it's like to remain humble. Jesus, the biggest celebrity to ever walk the earth, exemplified humbleness.

Let's face it, whether we're willing to admit it out loud or not, our culture has become Monster Academy, a worldly-accredited school beginning at birth and continuing for life. While many parents have great intentions of raising model citizens, what many actually create are little monsters. I must admit I am far from being an expert on parenting. However, I do spend time studying God's Word and what He has to say about raising children. My step-children were already adults living on their own when Diana and I married, but I now have three lovely grandchildren who spend a great deal of time in our home. I take my role as grandfather very seriously and consider it a gift from God to have the opportunity to speak into their little lives and experience a small portion of what it is like to parent. Diana and I try our best to avoid letting our grandchildren visit the campus of Monster Academy, but the campus life has a powerful draw and can easily fool even the wise into enrolling their children.

The world tells us giving material processions to our children is the best way to show love. Parents want children to have the cool toys marketers convince us they desperately need. Toys"R"Us hypnotizes parents early on with the toy gifting habit, which later turns into smartphones, designer clothes and cars. It's crazy how many young children are walking around with the latest iPhone. When I was a child, gifts were reserved for special occasions. Now I see some parents racing to the toy store weekly as if buying their children a new toy is a necessity for survival. Jesus warned us about collecting material possessions.

Do not lay up for yourselves treasures on earth, where moth and rust destroy and where thieves break in and steal, but lay up for yourselves treasures in heaven, where neither moth nor rust destroys and where thieves do not break in and steal. For where your treasure is, there your heart will be also.
(Matthew 6:19-21, ESV)

What God says about treasures compared to what many parents teach children is quite opposite. While we want the best for those precious young ones, many parents mistakenly give them everything they desire. Therefore, the spirit of Dr. Frankenstein is alive and well as parents train their children to desire an over abundance of things. Ironically, what they are actually doing is feeding the monster.

My close friend, Pete Orta, runs a ministry for displaced troubled teens and young adults called *In Triumph*. Similar to the majority of millennials in the U.S., many of the young folks who enter the *In Triumph* program possess an over abundance of entitlement. Pete shared with me how his personal research and experience led to discovering a key culprit to creating entitlement is the parental practice of over-rewarding children in their younger years. Many parents make the mistake of enticing children with gifts in order to motivate them to do things. Children eventually become performers in an effort to reap rewards. While rewarding a child to help potty train them may be effective and harmless, offering rewards for not mis-behaving can send the wrong message. Many children will learn to act badly in an effort to simply get the parent to offer a reward for good behavior. As a child attempts to maximize the receiving of rewards, the skill of manipulation is perfected. This reward and manipulation cycle is the foundation for creating a strong sense of entitlement in a child.

Another area where I see many parents struggling is with discipline. I'm probably opening a can of worms here, but I can't help but wonder what happened to spankings? While many politically correct parents will scream abuse, God tells us the following in Proverbs:

> *Whoever spares the rod hates his son, but he who loves him is diligent to discipline him.*
> (Proverbs 13:24, ESV)

No, it doesn't say, "beat your children to a pulp," but it does read like God is instructing us to use spankings to discipline. I have yet to meet a child who fears "time out" like I feared spankings as a kid. My parents didn't beat me, but the thought of getting a spanking filled me with fear and respect. Looking back, I don't think it was the pain of a spanking instilling fear, as my parents didn't spank very hard. Instead, I think it was more the humiliation of knowing I had let my parents down. Spankings normally took place immediately, shaking up my distorted thought process and bringing me back in line quickly. Conversely, using "time out" in place of spankings gives the child time to plan how they will outsmart the parent in the future. It's funny how society took "time out," which is used as a practice in sports for "taking a break to regroup, rest and plan in order to prevent a mistake from happening at a crucial point in a football, basketball or baseball game" and redirected its use for disciplining a child after a mistake has already happened. "Time out" may be a good tool to use when we see a child moving in the direction of misbehaving, but I would argue it's useless after the misbehavior has taken place.

My search for "reward your children" in the Bible came up empty. I did find the word reward throughout the Bible, but it is always associated with God giving out the rewards. I can't help but wonder if we humans try to take over God's role of "rewarding" and use it for our own self-gratifying purposes? Unfortunately, the way many parents now reward actually serves the purpose of feeding the ego. In an effort to make others feel good about themselves, we feel it necessary to reward. When the ego is fed, the person being rewarded appears to be happy and full of joy. Isn't that why every child gets a trophy in Little League whether they win or lose? That reward technique creates a temporary and false sense of joy. When the meaningless reward wears off, the child expects another even bigger reward for doing absolutely nothing.

Often times I fall into a similar reward trap with the artists we manage. In an effort to keep them happy, I feel the need to deliver some great news every time we talk. My personality is one that wants to please artists in order to receive affirmation that I'm a great manager. The potential danger is that I am actually enforcing an attitude of entitlement in the artists as I feed their egos. In fact, there was one particular artist we worked with whose sense of entitlement grew out of control. At the beginning of our relationship, I set up a weekly call to talk about what was going on in their personal life. They were young, and I felt a responsibility to mentor them as we developed their artist side. A few times, I made the mistake of delivering good news from the business side during a call originally designed to mentor. Our weekly mentoring call quickly morphed into a call where the artist expected good news about their career. Never had I felt more deserving of the Dr. Frankenstein title. A monster was being created on my watch.

chapter four:
LITTLE MONSTERS

Our company e-mail inbox is filled daily with submissions from people looking for management. We recently received the following e-mail with misspelled words and all:

> Hi my name is trevor and I really want to be a famous christain singer and im only 13 but I sing really nice. You can reach me at my phone at ###-###-#### hope to talk to you soon
>
> sincerly,
> trevor

As I read the e-mail, my heart became sad. Trevor doesn't just want to be a Christian singer. He wants to be a *famous* Christian singer. Somewhere in Trevor's life and his exposure to Christianity, he missed an important part of the message. God doesn't instruct us to seek fame. In fact, He tells us just the opposite when He says to go and tell all nations about Jesus to help make *Him* famous. I pray that God uses someone in Trevor's life to help him understand who God desires to become famous.

Our world has become a crazy place thanks to "me." Well illustrated in a song by Downhere titled "The Problem," the songwriter poetically explains how the problems in our world are a direct result of selfishness. What I love about the song is how it doesn't just preach at others. The songwriter recognizes the "me" in himself is also the problem. Wow! Wouldn't it be great if we started every day listening to the lyrics of that song? Recognizing "me" is the problem is a major step toward understanding why we need the grace and mercy God offers us.

"Me" is referred to as "the flesh" in the Bible. So what is the origin of "me"? Unfortunately, many years ago in the Garden of Eden, Satan tempted Eve with the fruit God had forbidden her and Adam to eat. He convinced Eve that eating the fruit would give her knowledge and, therefore, make her equal to God. The creator of the universe had given Adam and Eve life, placed them in paradise and given them dominion over every creature on earth; but it apparently wasn't enough. Adam, being the first "not so smart" man, also took a bite of the fruit, and the rest is history. Sadly, "me" was born.

> *Now the serpent was more crafty than any other beast of the field that the Lord God had made. He said to the woman, "Did God actually say, 'You shall not eat of any tree in the garden'?" And the woman said to the serpent, "We may eat of the fruit of the trees in the garden, but God said, 'You shall not eat of the fruit of the tree that is in the midst of the garden, neither shall you touch it, lest you die.'" But the serpent said to the woman, "You will not surely die. For God knows that when you eat of it your eyes will be opened, and you will be like God, knowing good and evil." So when the woman saw that the tree was good for food, and that it was a delight to the eyes, and that the tree was to be desired to make one wise, she took of its fruit and ate, and she also gave some to her husband who was with her, and he ate. Then*

the eyes of both were opened, and they knew that they were naked. And they sewed fig leaves together and made themselves loincloths.
(Genesis 3:1-7, ESV)

One of the early words a baby masters is "mine," which is actually a derivative of the word "me." What we help children understand about the word "mine" during the early thought development years helps determine how they will manage the monster gene. Those little babies are definitely cute, and it's quite fun to play the "mine" game with them, but imagine what could happen if we taught our children to associate the word "mine" with "yours"? Instead of teaching them to hold something tight saying, "mine," what if we taught them the meaning of the word "mine" was actually giving it to someone else? What if we changed the meaning of the word "mine" to "yours" and didn't replace the old word so the current meaning ceased to exist. Sadly, even if we changed the meaning of the word "mine," the monster gene and the spirit of "me" would still exist, thanks to the fall and this thing the Bible calls "the flesh." I think it's safe to assume God knows the spirit of "me" exists as He gives us wonderful instruction in the Bible on how to recognize and manage it.

But I say, walk by the Spirit, and you will not gratify the desires of the flesh. For the desires of the flesh are against the Spirit, and the desires of the Spirit are against the flesh, for these are opposed to each other, to keep you from doing the things you want to do.
(Galatians 5:16-17, ESV)

Do children really need a surprise every time they enter a store? Should we allow them to dictate what we serve them for dinner or what time they go to bed? How do we handle a child when they become demanding? Don't get me wrong. This grandfather's heart melts when I have the opportunity to give my grandchildren something they desire. Who knew the joy I would feel through buying a box of Lucky Charms for my grandson, because it's his favorite cereal? What happens though is when we give special things to children too often it becomes expected, and the specialness disappears. What was once intended as a special treat can quickly turn into expectation with an attitude of entitlement.

Our grandchildren became particular eaters due to us giving into food demands a bit too often. My wife's desire is to serve them whatever they want out of concern they won't eat. She is also "Super Nana," and spreading joy is knitted into her DNA. I subscribe more to the philosophy of "they will eat anything we serve them if they become hungry enough." While I may sound a bit mean, I'm also fairly quick to pull out ice cream if they eat the meal we put in front of them. When they are looking for snacks, Diana offers them healthy choices (like fruit), but I offer cookies and brownies. I say this not to judge or plead a case for which one of us is handling our grandchildren's desires the correct way, but instead to expose the tension adults deal with while teaching our little ones. However we approach the responsibility God bestows on us, we must teach them the dangers of "me" and the implications of feeding the monster.

While little monsters may be cute, we all know what happens when they grow up. They become big monsters, and the cuteness quickly disappears. They can make life very unpleasant for those around them, and even worse, is what they do to themselves through fostering a separation from God. While we can't make someone into who we want them to be, we can certainly give them biblical training in their early years. Teaching young children how to starve the monster is one of the greatest gifts we can pass along. Proverbs 22 sums that idea up in a single sentence.

Train up a child in the way he should go; even when
he is old he will not depart from it.
(Proverbs 22:6, ESV)

chapter five:
THE MONSTER EGO

God knows we all struggle with egos, which is why I think He is so specific about the subject in the Bible.

Pride goes before destruction, and a haughty spirit before a fall.
It is better to be of a lowly spirit with the poor than to
divide the spoil with the proud.
(Proverbs 16:18-19, ESV)

I also like the way this passage is translated in *The Message*, which reads:

First pride, then the crash—the bigger the ego, the harder the fall.
It's better to live humbly among the poor than to live it
up among the rich and famous.
(The Message)

When examining the verse, I notice the words *pride*, *haughty* and *ego* are viewed with high disdain by God. He warns those who don't live humbly that they are setting themselves up for destruction. I haven't met a single Christian artist who desires destruction or a fall, so I am compelled to wonder why so many willingly allow pride and ego to play a dominant role in their life. Are they reading His instructions and warnings? I find that in order for me to remain humble I must make reading the Bible a part of my daily regiment. Most new artists can tell you what Katy Perry eats for breakfast or what Chris Martin, Coldplay's front man, named his child; but they miss this giant warning from God? Ironically, this verse is found in Proverbs—one of the most popular books of the Bible—which makes it even harder to understand how a believer could miss it.

My beautiful wife, Diana, has an acronym she uses for ego: "Easing God Out." If that rings true, why would any Christian ever desire to have their ego boosted? In artist management, we deal with people full of insecurities. Most artists have some level of insecurity, and when they perform, they desire affirmation. *Did the audience like me? Did I do a good job? Did anyone notice that I sang a wrong lyric or note?* I often feel my role is to make them feel confident about their performance, so I pour on a bit of flattery. Before I even realize what I'm doing, I find myself in another territory the Bible warns about.

> *A man who flatters his neighbor spreads a net for his feet.*
> (Proverbs 29:5, ESV)

The phrase "spreads a net for his feet" is interpreted by many Bible scholars as "setting a trap for one's self." Every time I tell an artist how great they performed, I am offering food to the monster lurking inside and setting a trap for both the artist and myself. Unfortunately, I have found myself caught in that trap a few times and found it quite difficult to set myself free. Pouring on flattery can quickly make an artist difficult to work with, as they begin to think of themselves more highly than one should. Proverbs 29:5 presents a huge dilemma for a Christian artist manager, like myself. God calls me to act one way, but my desire to serve the artist pulls me in an opposing direction. God's way is clearly the right choice but one that could result in an extremely small artist roster. Thankfully, God has brought artists our way who also desire to walk under His instruction, and He weeds out those who prefer to serve their ego. While the artist roster pruning process may be painful at times, I rejoice in the final result as I know God is at work.

One artist came to us saying they wanted out of their management contract, because they had outgrown our company and our vision. At the time, they had sold very few records and had virtually no radio play. I found their statement, "We have outgrown your company and vision," to be an invalid assessment. My vision lines up with God's desire. Through helping artists get their music exposed to others, God can use it to change lives and draw people to Him. I don't think one can outgrow that. What I think they were actually saying was, "We want to be rock stars, and we don't think you have the desire to help us accomplish that." Their monster had been fed so well that it was roaring to take control. Sadly, once the monster is out, it has an insatiable appetite that will never be met. Regretfully, I helped feed that particular artist's monster by helping them land a record deal and an opening slot on a major tour. The tour was a "buy on" slot, which means their record label paid a large sum of cash to have them added to the tour. As a result of the tour, they picked up a few female fans, and their egos grew out of control. So much so that they began to believe they deserved a permanent and prominent position on a large-scale tour. Instead of being thankful for the slot they were blessed with, they began complaining about the extra time and opportunities other artists were given on the tour. Ironically, they had seen no radio success at that time, which normally drives the bids and slots from the larger tours. Putting the cart before the horse perfectly described their scenario, but they were convinced of a deserving greatness. The Apostle Paul has some poignant words for those who find themselves in that position.

> *I appeal to you therefore, brothers, by the mercies of God, to present your bodies as a living sacrifice, holy and acceptable to God, which is your spiritual worship. Do not be conformed to this world, but be transformed by the renewal of your mind, that by testing you may discern what is the will of God, what is good and acceptable and perfect. For by the grace given to me I say to everyone among you not to think of himself more highly than he ought to think, but to think with sober judgment, each according to the measure of faith that God has assigned.*
> (Romans 12:1-3, ESV)

Recently, I had a conversation with an artist whom I worked with during my record company days. This particular artist earned multiple Gold and Platinum records over the years and was one of the top artists in Christian music for the better part of a decade. I was sharing with him some of the ideas I was exploring for this book, and he brought up the idea of creative people being different and misunderstood. He explained how artists have insecurities others don't have to deal with, and they need affirmation in order to feel good about themselves. As I listened to what he had to say, part of me agreed, as I know many creative people who are insecure. Then I thought about what a misguided philosophy some have about creatives. Yes, God does create us all unique, and a creative person's thought process may be different than a more analytical person's. However, creatives are no more different or special than anyone else in God's eyes. Many non-creatives have similar insecurities and also need affirmation to feel good about themselves. This need can be present in both creatives and non-creatives and is nothing more than a hungry ego.

News flash: creatives don't get a free pass from God to be absorbed in the selfish need of ego stroking! I'm imagining a deafening gasp in the room as creatives read those words.. Yes, God made you with a creative mind, but He didn't intend for you to use it as an excuse to be consumed with self. Conversely, Jesus instructs us in Luke 9 to die to self.

And he said to all, "If anyone would come after me, let him deny himself and take up his cross daily and follow me. For whoever would save his life will lose it, but whoever loses his life for my sake will save it. For what does it profit a man if he gains the whole world and loses or forfeits himself?
(Luke 9:23-25, ESV)

There are multiple passages in the Bible encouraging believers to die to self. Here are a few more verses speaking directly about dying to self:

And those who belong to Christ Jesus have crucified the flesh with its passions and desires.
(Galatians 5:24, ESV)

For to me to live is Christ, and to die is gain.
(Philippians 1:21, ESV)

For whoever would save his life will lose it, but whoever loses his life for my sake and the gospel's will save it.
(Mark 8:35, ESV)

Even the Old Testament psalmist prays for help with "dying to self" in Psalm 119 when he prays:

> *Incline my heart to your testimonies, and not to selfish gain!*
> (Psalm 119:36, ESV)

Unfortunately, self absorption is not going to easily disappear thanks to our ancestors, Adam and Eve, and that enticing fruit they couldn't resist. What we can do though is recognize signs of ego and refuse to feed it. Resisting is impossible without God's help, but spending time in His Word gives one the strength to overcome. One of my favorite verses in the Bible reminds me of the strength Jesus gives.

> *I can do all things through him who strengthens me.*
> (Philippians 4:13, ESV)

That verse confirms creatives can flourish without affirmation from humans. God is the only source of affirmation one needs, and He gives it freely.

Artists aren't the only ones who battle with ego. I happen to know an artist manager who deals with ego daily. My need for approval and affirmation can be overwhelming at times. Even though I feel well balanced as an analytical creative, I like to know I'm rocking the world with accomplishment. When someone recognizes my accomplishments, I'm on a high, but I find it difficult to find peace when no one is acknowledging my work. Human desire to be known is visualized early in the Old Testament where it was the catalyst for the building of the Tower of Babel.

> *Now the whole earth had one language and the same words. And as people migrated from the east, they found a plain in the land of Shinar and settled there. And they said to one another, "Come, let us make bricks, and burn them thoroughly." And they had brick for stone, and bitumen for mortar. Then they said, "Come, let us build ourselves a city and a tower with its top in the heavens, and let us make a name*

for ourselves, lest we be dispersed over the face of the whole earth."
(Genesis 11:1-5, ESV)

My daily routine is similar to those who worked on the Tower of Babel, as I make myself busy gathering bricks and mortar in an attempt to build something large. My human desire is to be known as the greatest artist manager in the world, but I would be wise to note that a key phrase in the Tower of Babel story is "let us make a name for ourselves." God apparently didn't like their mantra and, therefore, decided to confuse them.

And the Lord came down to see the city and the tower, which the children of man had built. And the Lord said, "Behold, they are one people, and they have all one language, and this is only the beginning of what they will do. And nothing that they propose to do will now be impossible for them. Come, let us go down there and confuse their language, so that they may not understand one another's speech." So the Lord dispersed them from there over the face of all the earth, and they left off building the city. Therefore its name was called Babel, because there the Lord confused the language of all the earth. And from there the Lord dispersed them over the face of all the earth.
(Genesis 11:5-9, ESV)

While building artist careers and management companies may seem different than building a tower, the underlying intention can be the same. Our human desire to be celebrated for reaching greatness on our own is actually an attempt to Ease God Out. I think God included the story of the Tower of Babel in the Bible to help us understand how He views ego and the flawed human desire to be known.

chapter six:
MONSTERS OF ENTITLEMENT

Entitlement is rampant throughout the world but especially prevalent in American society. Many, including myself, believe entitlement is destroying the value system we once held dear in the U.S.A. So where was entitlement birthed? I have a theory as to the possible roots of entitlement in America. In the sixties and seventies there was quite a division between wealthy and middle class families. The wealthy families were the only ones who owned swimming pools, trampolines, nice cars and large homes. The middle class children growing up during that time had a strong desire to have things they saw wealthy families owning and, therefore, adopted a "whatever it takes to get it" attitude as they became adults and began having children of their own.

The middle class parents of the eighties made sure their children had access to material things once reserved for the wealthy. Swimming pools and trampolines began to pop up in middle class yards; designer clothes filled their closets, and large mortgages were taken on to buy bigger homes than families could actually afford. Debt became the norm. Children of the eighties developed a demanding attitude as expectations for material possessions increased.

creating MONSTERS

Families became double-income families with both mom and dad working in order to compete with those who had more. Americans began taking on more debt than could have ever been imagined. As we rolled into the nineties, the attitudes of children were noticeably different than those of the seventies. They expected Mom and Dad to provide them expensive clothes, cars and TVs for their bedrooms. In the next decade, some of the same behavior began to spill over into the lower class. Credit was easier to secure than ever before as credit card companies preyed on lower and middle income families. Most every kid in America had a mobile phone, the latest Nike shoes and cash in their pocket. Automobiles and homes could be financed for longer terms, making it possible to live way above one's means. The children who were given so much in the eighties were becoming adults and, now more than ever, expecting others to fund their lives. The Internet was created ushering in the philosophy of "anything, anywhere, anytime." American attitudes became "I want it here, now and immediately!" The idea of "no want should be impossible" was paraded in front of us by corporate marketers. Unfortunately, access to money often appears to be the panacea for "want" as it provides the means to turn "want" into "have." God addresses money throughout the Bible, warning us of its power. His instructions in Hebrews encourage us to stay away from the love of money.

Keep your life free from love of money, and be content with what you have, for he has said, "I will never leave you nor forsake you." So we can confidently say, "The Lord is my helper; I will not fear; what can man do to me?"
(Hebrews 13:5-6, ESV)

We all know what happened after 9/11 when the American financial bliss party came to a screeching halt. Reality of the enormous debt that Americans had accumulated quickly set in. Jobs were lost, houses and cars were repossessed by creditors and Americans found themselves in the middle of a huge recession. Entitlement was so deeply engrained that even the recession couldn't assuage it. Many Americans expected and demanded the government to bail them out of debt.

Entitlement and "me" are the heart and soul of the monster. Without those two things, the monster will find it difficult to survive. What we feed the monster in the early years will determine how big it becomes later in life.

While we can't remove the spirit of "me" that exists due to Adam and Eve's mistake, God tells us we can teach our children ways to squash it when it rears it's little head. Helping children understand the negative impact focusing on "me" brings to themselves and others is vital in their learning process. Creating scenarios for opportunities to experience the exhilarating feeling of giving is a great way to introduce them to focusing on others.

Every Christmas our church puts focusing on others into application. Our pastors encourage members to take a portion of what families would spend on Christmas for each other and, instead, give it away to others through our global mission fund. The motto is "Less under our tree means more for the world" It's really amazing to hear some of the stories parents share when they allow their children to decide what gift they will give up in order to send money to those in need. In addition to helping others around the world, the exercise of giving is sure to have an impact on the children in our church, which they'll carry on into adulthood.

I believe we can break the cycle of entitlement. In order to break the cycle, adults must change their attitude and expunge the emphasis we put on material possessions. I am encouraged when I see the younger generation getting more involved with social awareness campaigns and working on projects to help those in need. It is apparent good resides in the hearts of many. Unfortunately, I also see signs of the monster attempting to control the growing social awareness movement. Corporate marketers have discovered how attaching social awareness campaigns to their products is the new way into our pockets. TOMS is a great example. The company makes consumers feel good about purchasing its products because it's for a good cause; but ironically, it's also become a fashion statement. I'm not saying TOMS is evil, as I'm sure the company has good intentions, but the primary focus for most is on the fashion statement they make while wearing the fashionable shoes.

If we are diligent in teaching our children biblical truth on how God tells us to view treasures and giving, I believe we can starve the monster.

chapter seven:
MONSTERS OF MORE

We all deserve something, right? I know I find myself thinking the words "I deserve" quite often. When those words roll off my tongue, my sweet Diana quickly reminds me that we don't deserve a thing except death, according to what God tells us in Romans 6.

> *For the wages of sin is death, but the free gift of*
> *God is eternal life in Christ Jesus our Lord.*
> (Romans 6:23, ESV)

I am so incredibly thankful for the second half of that verse: "but the free gift of God is eternal life in Christ Jesus our Lord!" Wow! We deserve death, but God offers us eternal life with Him for free! Unfortunately, the world we live in doesn't always recognize the value of eternal life with Jesus as the ultimate gift. Marketers convince us we deserve more. Society tries to convince us success will bring more great things we deserve. Parents teach their children they deserve more and encourage them to chase it.

Thousands of books and conferences offer us the secrets to unlocking what we deserve.

One of the biggest ad campaigns ever launched was the campaign responsible for catapulting the McDonald's brand to great success forty-plus years ago with the slogan, "You Deserve a Break Today!" The motto has followed me through life well beyond the walls of McDonald's. Every time I feel exhausted or overwhelmed, "You Deserve A Break Today!" pops into my head. While I'm more inclined to head to Starbucks or Dairy Queen, I still feel like I deserve something. As much as I try to purge the words "I deserve" from my vocabulary, they continue to pop up. Thankfully, Diana's frequent reminders of what God teaches us also pop up seconds after the words leave my mouth. I'm then convicted, repent and remember Romans 6:23.

We have the sweetest grandchildren, and I am filled with a desire to protect them from developing a desire for more. Unfortunately, the sin nature they inherited from Adam and Eve and the consumer marketing wizards battle us hard for control of their minds. Our grandsons recently reached the age where the idea of receiving gifts for birthdays and Christmas becomes a big deal. I, of course, like to mess with their little minds through creative teaching moments. This past Christmas was a pivotal one for the boys. We put our Christmas tree up, and it really concerned the boys that there were no gifts under the tree. I had shopped early for Diana, so I intentionally made a huge deal out of placing two wrapped gifts for her under the tree. The boys went crazy with excitement thinking the gifts were for them. When they discovered their miscalculation, they were a bit disappointed. One of the boys became really upset stating with a devastating cry, "But we need presents!" Aha! The perfect teaching moment had just been laid in my lap. I sat the boys down to explain the true meaning of Christmas and gift giving. It seemed to sink in a bit, until we went on a trip to visit family in Atlanta and took some gifts to put under our Atlanta family's tree. Once again, we were hit with the devastating cry, "But we need presents!" So much for the wonderfully crafted teaching!

Diana and I discussed ideas on ways we could help assuage the boys' new insatiable desire for gifts. We decided to get them more involved in the gift-giving process. I had another gift for Diana I hadn't wrapped, so I called the boys to a secret meeting without Diana. I showed them the gift, let them help wrap it and made a big deal about how they couldn't tell Diana what was in the box. My plan was to help foster the spirit of giving. They took the wrapped gift to Diana, regularly teasing her, and telling her she had to wait till Christmas to open it. Our plan seemed to help the "but we need presents" attitude subside, and there was a new excitement for giving to someone else. Amazingly, on Christmas Day, the boys awoke and ran swiftly to the pile of gifts. As they were about to tear into an opening frenzy, out grandsons began frantically looking for the gift we had wrapped together for Diana. Before they opened one gift, they delivered the gift to Diana for her to open and summoned everyone in the room to watch. Seeing Diana open her gift was their priority for Christmas morning. My heart filled with joy to see our grandsons experience the exhilaration of giving to others.

I'm often surprised by the rampant attitude of "deserving more" amongst believers. Of all people, we should know we are undeserving of anything, as the Bible tells us so. Why then do we feel so deserving? I work with some godly artists, but I have also worked with others who were quickly led astray by the desire for more. I am amazed at how much time I have spent pacifying artists who think they deserve to be on a big tour or deserve to have great radio success.

I feel strongly we should strive to be excellent at the task God lays before us, but He is very capable of taking it from there. If we listen to God and give it our best, He will work His plan. After all, He is God, right? God's plan may not include a No. 1 radio single or an arena tour. His plan may be for an artist's song to reach only one person. It may sound crazy to spend $3,000-$4,000 recording a song and another $6,000 to work it to radio and only pick up one radio station, but isn't it worth $10,000 to help one person find Jesus?

chapter eight:
MONSTERS IN THE CLOSET

As our management company grew, so did our artist roster. When choosing artists, we look at talent, but more importantly, we take a close look at their heart for any signs of a monster. Thanks to the fall of Adam and Eve, we all have the monster gene; but the good news is the monster can be tamed through faith in Jesus and a heart for God. One of God's favorite people mentioned in the Old Testament was David. David's monster gene manifested itself through coveting, adultery and even murder; but his heart for God squelched the monster inside as he cried out to God for forgiveness.

Some people find a way to stuff the monster in a closet. If we then walk through life feeding the monster, the closet quickly becomes too small to contain it. One of the monster's favorite foods is jealousy. In the world of entertainment, jealousy surfaces quite often. We see success happening for others and can't help but wonder, *Why isn't that happening to me?* Not only do artists deal with jealousy, but managers deal with it in a similar way. I often find myself feeding the monster with jealousy. *Why do other management companies get the big breaks for their artists? Why can't we have that No. 1 hit? Isn't our song better than the ones finding success at radio?*

One monster-filled day, I decided to spend some time with God asking Him to bring success to our company. He led me to Proverbs 14:30.

A tranquil heart gives life to the flesh, but envy makes the bones rot.
(Proverbs 14:30, ESV)

The word *rot* stood out significantly and left me feeling a bit yucky with all the monster slime dripping off my body. What I heard from God would change my life forever. God confirmed His love for me and our company, but the Holy Spirit began to nudge me in a crazy direction. Suddenly, I felt the need to pray for success for our competition. When I recognize jealousy creeping in, I now stop and pray for success for those I'm jealous of. Yep. Praying for competitors' success is a difficult thing for us humans to do, but it purges the envy out of one's self fairly quickly. As the envy is purged out, something amazing happens. A peace like no other fills my soul. The tranquil heart God speaks of in Proverbs 14 feels so much better than rotting bones. In my newfound excitement, I even sent a few text messages out to those I felt jealousy toward to let them know I was praying for God to increase their territory and bless them. I'm sure some found it odd and wondered why I would be praying the prayer of Jabez for them, but I didn't care, as it felt exhilarating.

One artist I have the opportunity to work with has an incredible heart for God. Her heart for God is so evident through her relentless studying of His Word and her attentive listening to His voice. What's interesting is she still struggles with the monster gene just like the rest of us. Her monster is stuffed in the closet and often tries extremely hard to bust out. At times, I can hear the struggle with the monster in her voice; however, she allows God to take control, and He helps her slam the closet door shut with incredible force. When I see an artist dealing with the monster in this way, I'm encouraged that it is possible to use celebrity status to be an example for others.

After spending time contemplating ways to deal with the monster in the closet, a thought crossed my mind. What if tours, festivals and conferences added a monster closet to the backstage area? Something so opposite of the "green room," which is normally designed to pamper an artist. The monster closet would be a space where artists could spend time with God, cleaning off the monster slime. Feeling upset about what little time you were given for soundcheck or how much of the stage the other artists took up with their gear? Why not spend a few minutes in the monster closet? Maybe there's a box in the closet where artists could leave anonymous complimentary and encouraging notes for other artists on the show or for the sound and production crew? No need to feel embarrassed for entering the closet, because exiting the closet and leaving the monster behind would be celebrated by all! The notes of encouragement could be read to everyone on the tour during the devotion time that some Christian tours include on their daily schedule. Imagine the potentially positive effects a monster closet could have on a tour or festival. Imagine what effects a monster closet at home could have on ordinary families as they navigate life.

chapter nine:
MONSTERS OF ROCK

The eighties ushered in one of the biggest egos the world had ever seen. David Lee Roth took the world by storm. With the success of Van Halen, the band he fronted, Roth was elevated to the top of the celebrity food chain. He referred to his persona as "Dave's World." Flamboyant pop rock ruled the radio airwaves while MTV offered an inside look at the extreme decadence surrounding it. Possessing a bigger than life ego became acceptable in American society for the first time. The days of polite entertainers with proper etiquette were tossed aside in leu of the new "me" society. A foundation of self-worship was laid for future rock stars, professional athletes and reality TV stars. Hence, the Monsters of Rock were born!

Working with celebrities in mainstream music was interesting, but it presented many challenges. Some handled fame well and were quite pleasant to be around, but many of the artists I worked with were difficult. At Capitol Records, we were instructed to keep the artists happy at all costs. Many of the artists were humble at the beginning of their career but would quickly turn into demanding jerks with the slightest bit of success. We all complained and despised working with them once they became jerks, but ironically, we helped create the jerks.

I had the opportunity to work with Garth Brooks in the early days of his career and through the explosion of success that put him on arena stages making him the top artist in the world. He was an extremely kind man in the early years. Garth's success was a major contributor to Capitol's bottom line, and utilizing his business savvy, he leveraged that contribution to the max. Shortly after his huge hit, "Friends in Low Places," Garth aggressively renegotiated his record deal. The aggressive negotiations became a catalyst for discourse with the record label's upper management, leading Garth to distance himself from all label employees. He was never unkind to me, but there was definitely a change in his personality. Upper management at the label suggested he had developed a dark side, but in reality, I think he probably felt misunderstood. Garth's desire was to break every sales, radio and touring record in music history. He planned events that had never been done in the entertainment business and pulled most of them off with great success. I couldn't help but wonder how tough it must have been for him to battle the monster gene. Millions of people around the world worshipped the man. All he had to do was walk on stage, touch his hat, and 100,000 people would go nuts! How can the human mind even begin to process that level of adoration in a non-"me" way? Britney Spears, Justin Bieber and Miley Cyrus have given us front row seats to witness the damaging effects worshipping young humans can have. Ironically, most of us are guilty of feeding the celebrities' monsters as we pour out our worship toward them—a worship that God tells us should be reserved for Him.

After my career move to the Christian side of music, I expected artists to be different. There were indeed many godly artists I worked with, but some of the artists expected to be given preferential treatment, much like mainstream artists I had worked with. While their demands and expectations were coated with a smile and a godly-laced delivery, they no doubt wanted special treatment. If those artists found unsatisfactory representation in retail stores, label employees would catch grief from the artist's camp. While the messenger was usually the artist manager, it was apparent the artists were driving the complaints. The Target, Wal-Mart, Best Buy, Tower Records and Lifeway stores in Nashville were high-profile stores, as they were located in the artists' backyards. For some reason, those same stores were the toughest places to maintain satisfactory inventory levels. If one of our artists walked into Target and didn't find their record, we would most certainly hear about it. So much so that we began visiting those stores daily, taking in free product to insert into the shelves and end caps in an effort to guarantee our titles were in stock.

Our shelf stocking practice kept the artists happy, even though they ultimately lost money on the sales of CDs, which were never purchased by the retail store. It probably wasn't one of the wisest financial decisions for our company, but it kept the artists' egos and management off our backs. Everyone was happy except our competitor labels who couldn't figure out how we were able to get certain titles in Target or Best Buy. While it isn't one of my proudest career moments, I have to chuckle when I picture a cashier at Target trying to ring up a CD that Target's corporate office never purchased or set up in their system. In a similar fashion, we would regularly visit the Wal-Mart stores and move our titles to big end caps in the music section. One day while playing the Wal-Mart end cap title switch game, I was confronted by an employee who managed the Wal-Mart music section. In an effort to let me know he was on to our shenanigans, he informed me that the reps from our competitors would be in the next day to do the same with their titles, hence negating my efforts. Extremely embarrassed and convicted, it hit me how silly my actions were. Here I was, a vice president for a Christian record company, using ridiculous extreme measures to feed the monster.

When we started our management company, I knew we didn't want any "monsters of rock" on our roster. Even with close examination, a few of those artists somehow slipped through. The monster will manifest quickly as the artist experiences any success. One particular artist we worked with ended up on a large tour. Even though their record company paid a large sum of money to buy their way onto the tour, they quickly adopted an attitude of entitlement. We spent a great deal of time before the tour preparing the artist for the reality they would face when the big tour ended and they had to return to the norm of playing for smaller audiences. Leaping from playing for 100 people a night to playing for arena-size audiences of 10,000-15,000 can seriously mess with an artist's mind if they don't remain humble and deeply rooted in God's Word. We examined earlier what the Bible says about pride in Proverbs 16 and how it leads to destruction. Proverbs 11 reiterates the results of pride but also tells us the benefit of humbleness.

> *When pride comes, then comes disgrace,*
> *but with the humble is wisdom.*
> *(Proverbs 11:2, ESV)*

Wisdom is one of the greatest gifts God gives us, as it keeps us in step with His plan and gives us the ability to navigate difficult encounters in life. Unfortunately for all involved, that particular artist was unsuccessful at remaining humble and keeping the monster in the closet. The monster manifested itself in such a way that our relationship was strained. As I struggled with disappointment, thinking we failed in teaching them humbleness, God reminded me that I am only an instrument He uses. While He may use us to plant seeds, He is ultimately in control, and it is His job to take it from there.

Another artist we worked with was blessed with a huge opportunity to play a high-profile festival in London with Neil Young, Bruce Springsteen and The Dave Matthews Band. I must admit that weekend was one of my most memorable weekends in the music business. We were treated like rock stars and hung out with an elite list of celebrity artists. I was having a hard enough time keeping my own monster in the closet, but my job for the weekend was to look after this particular artist. The artist and I shared a beautiful room in a luxury hotel overlooking Hyde Park. I stepped out for a few minutes, and when I returned to the room, there was a nice little shocking surprise waiting for me. This artist had taken every square inch of space in our room for his clothes. Every closet, chair and dresser drawer were full of his things. I honestly don't know how he managed to pack all of those clothes into one bag. As I entered the room and noticed he had even taken over the night stand on my side of the room and had clothes draped on my bed, I realized we might have a problem. His words? "Sorry man, I know I took up all the space in the room, but I have a lot of stuff. I am the artist, you know." There was no offer to move anything. In that moment, I knew we had a rock star on our hands and our business relationship would probably be challenging.

Over the years, Diana and I have put a rock star litmus test in place. Although it's not totally fool proof, it definitely gives us a quick insight into how an artist manages the monster. When we are looking at new artists, we have them stay a night or two with us in our home. During their stay, we closely examine a few things. The most important thing we want to know is whether or not they are looking *to be* served or looking *to* serve. That's easy to assess fairly quickly. Do they grab their plates and offer to help with dishes after a meal? Do they treat the room they are staying in like a hotel room, leaving a mess for someone else to clean? Not that we expect guests in our home to clean, but it certainly shows a lot about person's character if they offer to help. Some artists have been extremely grateful for the stay, while others treat our home as if it were a hotel with maids and room service.

I can remember one particular artist who was extremely narcissistic. Diana had been slaving in the kitchen cooking and cleaning for him for several days. One evening, we looked out on the porch and had to chuckle with amazement. This artist was stretched out on the chaise lounge on our porch, relaxing as if he were in paradise waiting for someone to serve his every need. All he needed was someone fanning him with a giant palm branch to complete the paradisal scene. That seemed like a pretty good sign that he would be trouble down the road. On the other hand, some artists have shown up with gift baskets or left thank you notes showing extreme gratitude. When we see those traits, we are encouraged.

What does God think about those who seek to be rock stars in Christian music? While I can't speak for God, Jesus' words teach us about seeking high places of honor.

> *When you are invited by someone to a wedding feast, do not sit down in a place of honor, lest someone more distinguished than you be invited by him, and he who invited you both will come and say to you, "Give your place to this person," and then you will begin with shame to take the lowest place. But when you are invited, go and sit in the lowest place, so that when your host comes he may say to you, "Friend, move up higher." Then you will be honored in the presence of all who sit at the table with you. For everyone who exalts himself will be humbled, and he who humbles himself will be exalted.*
> (Luke 14:8-11, ESV)

Jesus himself modeled His words when He washed the disciples' feet. The most deserving rock star of all time lowered Himself to wash the dirt off people's feet. As He was washing their feet, He offered some great wisdom:

> *When he had washed their feet and put on his outer garments and resumed his place, he said to them, "Do you understand what I have done to you? You call me Teacher and Lord, and you are right, for so I am. If I then, your Lord and Teacher, have washed your feet, you also ought to wash one another's feet. For I have given you an example, that you also should do just as I have done to you. Truly, truly, I say to you, a servant is not greater than his master, nor is a messenger greater than the one who sent him."*
> (John 13:12-16, ESV)

Reading those words should lead believers to conclude that rock star attitudes have no place in Christian music if the music indeed exists to honor and glorify God. Jesus' words "for I have given you an example" don't appear to be shrouded in mystery. If we are to follow His example, why would any Christian artist adopt a rock star attitude? He also gives us very poignant words in Proverbs.

Everyone who is arrogant in heart is an abomination to the Lord;
be assured, he will not go unpunished.
(Proverbs 16:5, ESV)

Why do Christian managers, booking agents and record labels create environments that foster rock star attitudes? Why does the Christian music industry create, promote and support award shows and red carpet events that emulate the mainstream industry by rewarding people for human achievements in record sales, airplay and popularity? I believe the answer lies in the existence of the monster gene or what the Bible calls "the flesh." The monster seeks money, power and fame and is quite clever at making even Christians feel good about themselves as they feed it. Conversely, if we cease to feed the monster, the rock star attitude will not survive.

chapter ten:
PARENTAL MONSTERS

When babies are born, parents begin to dream. Immediately upon birth, fantasies of their child accomplishing great things begin swirling around in their minds. *Could we have just given birth to the future President of the United States? Maybe the next Michael Jordan, Peyton Manning or Derek Jeter? What if our child discovers the cure for cancer?* Realizing our shortcomings as humans, we want our children to find the greatness we failed to achieve. I remember sitting around with our kids, as grandchild number one was on the way, and trying to help them find the perfect name. Our litmus test was how the name would sound when the announcers read the starting line-up for any sporting or entertainment event over the PA. Next batter up... "insert potential name" Ladies and gentlemen... "insert potential name." It was quite the fun name-picking exercise, but deep down inside, we really hoped our grandchildren would find greatness in life. Finding greatness is a valid wish for anyone, but is greatness measured by fame, wealth or accomplishments? Doesn't God think every single human being is great at birth? Yet most of us still feel the need to break out the measuring stick of

creating MONSTERS

success to create our own scale of greatness. The monster desires to drive the success agenda.

When I first met Diana, I was a bit intimidated. She was mother to a teenage celebrity who happened to be one of the top-selling artists at the record company I worked for. I don't know how or why God brought us together to become husband and wife, but He did, and I'm eternally grateful. The beautiful thing is how I had an opportunity to watch Diana in action as a mother years before there was any romantic interest. Maybe watching her operate as a beautiful, loving mother and seeing Jesus work through her stirred my attraction to her. She possesses a heart of gold like no other human I've met.

Shortly after we were married, I ran across an article written by a misinformed writer. He had only seen Diana from afar and totally misread her as he compared her to other celebrity stage moms the press likes to write about. I had worked extensively with Diana, witnessing the exact opposite of this writer's description of her. Naturally, I took it upon myself to contact the writer and share with him the truth about how Diana beautifully carried out her role as a celebrity's mother. Diana took on the role of protector and mentor for her daughter. She was always present with her daughter during the teenage years, in an effort to walk out her role as mother. Diana traveled with her daughter, as she didn't think it was wise to allow a teenage girl to travel alone or to travel on promotional trips with adult men. Often, you would find Diana in the background behind-the-scenes just being Mom. Never once did I see her trying to grab the spotlight or pushing her daughter to get on stage. For years, I have tried to get Diana to write a book about her life as a celebrity's mom, but to this day, she doesn't want to take the risk of moving into the spotlight.

In the early days of our management company, we were presented with an opportunity to work with a young artist. There was a mom involved, and I thought Diana would be the perfect mentor to help the mom walk out her motherly role in a healthy way. After all, Diana had walked with her daughter through a career of Platinum-selling records, major movie roles and large tours. She had seen the good, the bad and the impact a career on stage can have on a young person. Unfortunately, the mom we encountered felt she was already equipped for the journey. She was ready to bully the world into making her child a star. We encountered Super Stage Mom! Interestingly, Jesus encountered what may have been one of the first stage moms, but He quickly shut her down.

> *Then the mother of the sons of Zebedee came up to him with her sons, and kneeling before him she asked him for something. And he said to her, "What do you want?" She said to him, "Say that these two sons of mine are to sit, one at your right hand and one at your left, in your kingdom." Jesus answered, "You do not know what you are asking. Are you able to drink the cup that I am to drink?" They said to him, "We are able." He said to them, "You will drink my cup, but to sit at my right hand and at my left is not mine to grant, but it is for those for whom it has been prepared by my Father." And when the ten heard it, they were indignant at the two brothers. But Jesus called them to him and said, "You know that the rulers of the Gentiles lord it over them, and their great ones exercise authority over them. It shall not be so among you. But whoever would be great among you must be your servant, and whoever would be first among you must be your slave, even as the Son of Man came not to be served but to serve, and to give his life as a ransom for many."*
> (Matthew 20:20-28, ESV)

Sadly, the mom we worked with blew an opportunity to have Diana, mother of an international celebrity, help her navigate her child's music career in a beautiful way. Instead, the mom's desire for the spotlight and success fed the monster.

As we embarked on our journey with the young artist, we saw early on that the mom wanted success as much as her child. Every show, she was front and center ensuring that every person in the venue knew she was the artist's mother. Even as the artist entered their twenties, we couldn't have a call without Mom lurking in the background listening to every word. I would often hear her whispering on our calls, telling the artist what to say. She would monitor and answer e-mails from us and others as if she was the artist. Mom controlled every move, rendering the artist powerless over their own life and career. The situation was one of the unhealthiest parent/child relationships I've experienced in the music business. Her actions were disguised under smiles in public, but behind the scenes, it was not a pretty picture. We spent some time on the road with the mom and her husband, and truth was revealed to us in a big way. Most mornings, she would begin the day belittling her husband. He was a kind man and passively excused her behavior. Both Diana and I were extremely uncomfortable and embarrassed for her husband as we drove down the road listening to his wife put him down. We wanted out of the car, and we actually almost asked to be dropped off during one of the episodes. Those actions go against everything God's Word teaches regarding how wives are called to treat and respect their husbands. Life in their home had to be miserable at times for both her husband and child. I would speculate there are deep insecurity issues from the mom's childhood that caused that behavior to surface. Regardless, the way she treats her family and others is extremely unhealthy and the perfect recipe for feeding the monster.

The artist's mom portrayed her child as tough, but as soon as her child walked off stage, she was there to tell him everything he did wrong. We would see the disappointment in the young artist's face as he listened to Mom roll through a list of mistakes. The mom actually wanted us to do the same by critiquing the show immediately after the performance, but we refused. She claimed her child welcomed the criticism, but I don't think there is a parenting expert in the world who would agree those methods are healthy parenting. We prayed regularly for

God to reveal the unhealthy practices to the mom and the artist.

The mom eventually attempted to treat us like she treated her child and husband, constantly complaining about what was not happening in her child's career in an effort to make us feel as though we didn't measure up. Ironically, we had delivered a nice platform for her child through securing a record deal, a booking agent and big tour opportunities. It apparently wasn't enough. This mom's insatiable appetite for the stage and success was impossible to satisfy. My desire to please allowed me to get pulled into her craziness at times, but I quickly realized the negative effects. After spending hours of the day trying to assuage the artist's mom, I would find myself treating Diana unkindly in the evenings. Once I recognized the negative effect this unhealthy mom was having on me, I refused to allow it to continue.

When parents act in toxic ways, like the mom we encountered, it's obvious the monster is present. Once the monster controls Mom, controlling the child is an easy task. Unfortunately, residual effects can often surface later in life causing problems with the child's career, future marriage and other key relationships. Living life on a stage presents enough problems to a young artist as it is, but mixing in an unhealthy parental relationship creates fertile conditions for the monster to thrive.

chapter eleven:
MONSTERS OF WORSHIP

> *But the hour is coming, and is now here, when the true worshippers will worship the Father in spirit and truth, for the Father is seeking such people to worship him.*
> (John 4:23, ESV)

That verse makes it pretty clear that God is looking for worshippers. Most Christians have their own opinions on what it means to worship. Some think singing reverent hymns is the only true way to worship God, while others think shouting worship songs from a big stage or a frenzy of interpretive dancing is the only true way. Funny thing is, most of our ideas of worship are centered around "me" and what makes "me" feel good. Just as guilty as others, I have found myself driving away from a church service critiquing the worship. "I just didn't feel it today" has rolled off my tongue more often than I care to admit.

Many of us modern worshippers were captivated when we first heard Martin Smith of Delirious sing "I Could Sing of Your Love Forever" or

Darlene Zschech's "Shout To The Lord." Without intending to dismiss anyone's true experience with worshipping God, I wonder if what we feel is sometimes confused with the emotion that an incredibly written song naturally stirs. I definitely felt an overwhelming swell of emotion the first hundred times I sang "Shout To The Lord" in church, but I feel a similar emotion when I hear Celine Dion belt out "My Heart Will Go On." I truly believe God breathes great songs through people, but is the emotion we seek from singing them about "me" and how it makes "me" feel, or is it about how it makes God feel? The monster desires to control our worship in an effort to divert it away from its intended purpose of glorifying God.

The demanding worship experience that many modern-day Christians have adopted gave birth to the modern-day "worship leader"—not just some person on stage leading songs, but a "true worship leader." You know, the guy in skinny jeans with a cool guitar, hip hairstyle and endearing prayer voice. We once had a worship leader at my church who added a slight British accent to his singing and talking voice. It sounds cool to some and gives that Delirious/Hillsong vibe, but I can't help but laugh inside every time I hear it, wondering what a British person might think if they heard it. Personally, I enjoy being led by a hip modern worship leader with lyrics projected on a screen much more than some staunch guy in a suit waving his hand around like a symphony conductor. Am I wrong to allow personal preference to determine the way I worship, or should I put more emphasis on who I am called to worship? If my desires are to worship the Creator, shouldn't I still be able to do that with whatever style of worship leader I encounter?

The Christian music industry and demanding worshippers have contributed greatly to the creation of the Monsters of Worship. Rock star worship leaders with large egos abound. I often hear stories of the battles that go on behind the scenes of churches over who gets selected to sing on the worship team each week. While there are plenty of incredible churches with authentic, godly worship leaders and worship teams, I also know many worship leaders and musicians struggle with the monster gene. Yep. Thanks to Adam and Eve and the fall, the monster gene is in every single one of us.

Nashville is full of super talented musicians, so one can attend any church in the area and expect a high caliber of musicianship. There is one church in Nashville well known for its incredible choir. That particular church had to install a policy a few years back requiring one to be a member of the church for a year before being allowed to join their choir. Apparently, vocalists were attending the church and joining the choir in an effort to showcase their voice to the music industry professionals who attend the church. I often wonder what it would be like if the super talented singers and musicians were filled with the desire to spread out across the nation, blessing churches in rural towns with their gifts, as opposed to cocooning in Nashville in hopes of being discovered by the music industry? We have several worship leaders at our church and, recently, our favorite moved to South Carolina. My initial emotion upon hearing the news of his move was extreme sadness. But then I realized how great it is that such a talented musician would leave the comforts of Music City and share his gift in South Carolina. It won't be easy for him to co-write and record from South Carolina, but what a huge blessing for his new church family!

Hopefully, my worship leader friends don't think I am attempting to paint them in a bad light. My intentions are to point out the pressures we worshippers create with our demanding needs. Many worship leaders have a self-imposed measurement of how effective they are at leading worship. If they don't feel the energy coming back from the audience through loud singing and hands lifted high in the air, they feel like a failure. Fear of failure is a weapon the enemy uses to take out worship leaders. What a difficult balancing act for worship leaders. I don't think most of us who sit in churches on Sunday realize how difficult of a task it is for our worship leaders. The monster is always lurking in the shadows, hoping to be fed. Often times, the demanding congregations are the ones picking out the food to serve the monster. It's disheartening to hear stories from worship leaders about the negative notes and feedback they receive on Monday mornings regarding their "performance" on Sunday. I don't think God intends it to be a performance. Isn't worship supposed to be a beautiful celebration of glorifying Him?

During my time working in the international department at Word Entertainment, I had the opportunity to visit Hillsong Church in Australia. Hillsong Music was topping the CCLI chart, the worship music chart that measures songs being sung in the churches every Sunday across the U.S. Being a self-proclaimed "modern worshipper," I was super excited to visit the church at the center of the modern movement. Upon arrival, there was a V.I.P. seat reserved for me. My special seat was located near the president of Hillsong Music with a perfect view of the worship platform. The thought, *I must be a special worshipper this morning* actually ran through my mind as the monster of worship began to stir inside. What I would experience that day was a little different than expected, but it would change my view of worship forever.

The Hillsong campus was amazingly beautiful, and the worship center was arena size, but what I experienced there was something incredibly genuine. No fake accents (of course they didn't need them), no fog machines or laser light show, just genuine worshippers. I instantly realized how Americans had taken something so genuine and turned it into a rock show. Don't get me wrong, there was plenty of energy on the stage, but something felt so pure. Darlene Zschech didn't overtake the platform as some kind of rock star. Instead, it was a worship team experience. I think it was actually her sister who took the worship leader role that morning. On the long plane ride back to the U.S., I pondered the thought of how we Americans took something God birthed in Australia and super-sized it into "monster worship" for America. It's obvious God had big plans for "Shout To The Lord" and the Hillsong movement around the world, but it manifested itself so differently in the U.S. What I saw in the U.S. was more about how much emotion the worship leader could create with the song. If we, the church audience, didn't get to sing "Shout To

The Lord" during the worship service, it was a disappointing Sunday. I would actually hear people complain when the song wasn't sung in a service. God has definitely used and continues to use "Shout To The Lord" in a mighty way around the globe. However, I can't help but think how many monsters of worship used it for self-gratification as opposed to glorifying God.

God created us to worship in ways that may seem crazy to others. He wants our unabashed worship poured out toward Him. David exemplified just that when he danced with all his might in celebration and worship to God. So much so that his wife was embarrassed and displeased.

And David danced before the Lord with all his might. And David was wearing a linen ephod. So David and all the house of Israel brought up the ark of the Lord with shouting and with the sound of the horn. As the ark of the Lord came into the city of David, Michal the daughter of Saul looked out of the window and saw King David leaping and dancing before the Lord, and she despised him in her heart.
(2 Samuel 6:14-16, ESV)

And David returned to bless his household. But Michal the daughter of Saul came out to meet David and said, "How the king of Israel honored himself today, uncovering himself today before the eyes of his servants' female servants, as one of the vulgar fellows shamelessly uncovers himself!" And David said to Michal, "It was before the Lord, who chose me above your father and above all his house, to appoint me as prince over Israel, the people of the Lord—and I will celebrate before the Lord. I will make myself yet more contemptible than this, and I will be abased in your eyes. But by the female servants of whom you have spoken, by them I shall be held in honor." And Michal the daughter of Saul had no child to the day of her death.
(2 Samuel 6:20-23, ESV)

Looking at those verses, I determined that it really isn't my place to judge anyone's style of worship. The story gives us a picture of genuine, spontaneous worship. David's worship was so pure that the monster reared its head through Michal, his wife, as she attempted to condemn him. Reading the last verse of the story ("And Michal the daughter of Saul had no child to the day of her death.") leads me to believe that God was displeased with Michal's desire to control David's worship. So much so, that He prevented her from receiving the honor of bearing a child with David. Genuine worship squashed the monster that so badly wanted to control David's style of worship.

chapter twelve:
PLATFORM VS. STAGE

    A platform is a tool God gives us humans to use for making Him famous. The size, shape and nature of the platform varies based on our individual calling. A fast food drive-thru window, a corporate board room, a meal wagon serving the homeless, a major league sports field, or an arena concert for twenty thousand people can all serve the same purpose of spreading the Gospel of Jesus. What we do with the platform is a huge responsibility. Unfortunately, the monster recognizes the power of the platform and desires to control it. The larger the platform, the harder the monster will fight to own it.

    I recently ran into a former pastor, mentor and friend of mine. Dave served as an accountability pastor for several artists and musicians over the years. As we were talking, he mentioned a successful Christian artist recently came to him concerned she had become a diva as a result of her music success. She was seeking advice on how to change. He, of course, told her she needed to ask forgiveness from anyone she had wronged, but then he gave her a huge nugget of wisdom every artist should hear. Dave explained to this artist how a platform becomes a stage the second an artist allows the focus to be on themselves. If an artist finds themselves overly concerned about how well they controlled the audience, how cool or beautiful they looked on stage or how many screaming fans they have, it might be a good time to pause and examine their purpose. When the platform becomes a stage for a Christian, they have most likely stepped out of God's purpose for their life. Wow! That's simple truth for anyone, no matter what platform they have been given, but so appropriate for those in the entertainment field. There is an intentional art to striving for excellence while maintaining God's purpose. Staying connected to God through prayer and studying His Word is a great way to maintain that purpose.

While the sound equipment, lights and backdrop may look like a stage, they are merely tools God provides some to use for their platform. Artists, musicians and worship leaders can use the tools to draw in an audience, but where they take the audience once they draw them in is key. Therein lies the tension for an artist manager—how to balance helping the artist strive for excellence without helping them turn the platform into a self-gratifying stage. Platforms come in all shapes and sizes, and God does provide bigger platforms for some. No matter the size of the platform, an artist must create an environment that draws an audience in to listen. In order to maximize larger platforms, artists must operate at a high level of excellence on par with the top entertainers in the world.

As we develop artists and help them create a "drawing people in" environment, I often find myself using words like *performance, stage presence* and *production quality*. Those words can be extremely dangerous when used or taken in the wrong context. For me, praying for wisdom in coaching artists is vital. It is also important to be equally yoked with artists who are spiritually likeminded. Discerning whether an artist is seeking platform or stage in their heart can be tricky, as most learn to articulate with "Christianese" early in their career. I have found that actions reveal the true desire of the heart. When I hear an artist complain about having the opening slot or not having as much time for their set as other artists are given, I take their words as a good indicator that they are focused primarily on the stage. We are all human, so it would be silly to expect artists to never have thoughts of stage in their mind, which is the very reason artists should surround themselves with accountability and stay in God's Word.

Over the years, I have heard artists say they are a "Christian entertainer," not a minister. While I partly understand what they are trying to say, the distinction doesn't exist within God's Word. They may not be great speakers, but they can still minister as entertainers. Jesus calls *all* of us, not some of us, to be ministers who carry out the Great Commission.

> *Go therefore and make disciples of all nations, baptizing them in the name of the Father and of the Son and of the Holy Spirit.*
> (Matthew 28:19, ESV)

If those are Jesus' instructions, doesn't it make sense that He would want us to use the platform He gives us to carry out the Great Commission? When it's misused to promote "me," the platform, instead, transforms into an obstacle for leading others to Christ.

Another interesting observation are those artists who are so adamant about not being labeled a "Christian artist." When interviewed by media, they say everything possible to get the interviewer off the subject of Christianity. In my opinion, that's monster talk at its finest! I can certainly understand not wanting to be quarantined to the small Christian music genre section in mainstream retail stores, but why would any Christian ever avoid being associated with Jesus? Haven't they read how Peter felt when he heard the rooster crow a third time? I have heard the argument that it's the association with the sub-par produced Christian music they wish to avoid. Others avoid talking about their Christian faith in an effort to have world appeal, allowing them to reach a larger audience. Imagine a loud buzzer sound as I throw the penalty flag here! I don't recall Jesus cloaking His Messiah-ness in order to attract the attention of a crowd. Masses were drawn to His heavenly aroma and amazing teaching. What does Jesus say about denying Him?

> *And I tell you, everyone who acknowledges me before men, the Son of Man also will acknowledge before the angels of God, but the one who denies me before men will be denied before the angels of God.*
> (Luke 12:8-9, ESV)

Those words read pretty clear to me. I know I don't want to be denied by God.

Over the years, I have heard many Christian artists cite U2 as the artist they wish to emulate. U2 has indeed made great music and impacted the world immensely. The band didn't use the Christian music industry as a back door to mainstream success, as I see so many artists attempt to do. Instead, they went about playing music, and God gave them a large platform, which they choose to use to spread His message of love. Bono has been quite wise in the way he uses the platform to share the Gospel. Yes, he dropped the F-bomb on national TV, which I'm not endorsing, but the fruit he bears in everyday life with humanitarian efforts speaks volumes to the world. His love for God and other humans appears to be genuine and is obviously a major priority in his life. He also uses his songwriting gift to craft a Christian message throughout many of his lyrics. Unfortunately, many young artists who wish to emulate U2, lock in on the F-bombs but overlook the God-loving, humanitarian story. We then end up with a bunch of self-professed "cool" Christian musicians in search of the stage, running around dropping F-bombs and claiming it's their clandestine way of sharing Jesus with the world. The platforms of artists who are lost in that way crumble as their stage is erected.

Imagine the possibilities when one focuses on the platform God gives them instead of the platform He gives someone else. While God does call us to excellence in whatever we do, attempting to deliver huge worldly audiences is taking over God's role. When He desires an artist to have a massive audience,

He will deliver the massive audience. Ask Bart Millard from MercyMe what God did with his blatant song about Jesus a few years back. Through God's orchestration, "I Can Only Imagine" found its way into heavy rotation on mainstream radio stations around the country. The Texas mainstream radio station's decision to play the song for the first time wasn't planned by any record company. A listener called in and requested the song during a request show. Listener response was great and grabbed the radio station's attention. God then gave MercyMe's record company the vision, wisdom and tools to work His plan from there. The success of "I Can Only Imagine" was so far outside the normal lanes of working a Christian single that it can't be classified as anything other than God's divine plan.

We are currently working with an artist who has the ability to craft lyrics with a biblical message in a way that doesn't offend most mainstream audiences. This particular artist is signed to a record label who chose to work him to mainstream radio before working his music to Christian radio. Unlike many Christian artists with mainstream stars in their eyes, this artist's primary goal is to honor God through music. We have worked carefully to help him craft a message for the media that allows him to speak to the world in a way that encourages them to open their hearts and minds to the message of Jesus. The task comes with a huge responsibility, and if done wrong, could easily alienate believers and non-believers. Although his mainstream publicist gets a bit nervous when he refers to God, I'm thankful the artist isn't willing to deny his faith in order to deliver the message. Ironically, his music is being played on mainstream stations in major markets across the U.S. allowing him to share his faith on worldly platforms. It's amazing how right that feels and how honored I am to be a part of his team.

When I see artists avoiding association with Jesus or seeking the spotlight on stage, it is apparent the monster is alive and well. Pursuit of fame, success and money is not of God. His purpose for all believers is that we use whatever platform He gives us to make Him famous.

chapter thirteen:
SOCIAL NETWORK MONSTERS

How many followers do you have? It's a question artists must be prepared to answer with a significant number in order to be validated by the current music industry. The number of "followers," "friends" and "likes" one has on Twitter, Facebook and Instagram now determines one's net worth to industry gatekeepers.

I must admit I am guilty of being at the forefront of the social network movement, which perpetuated social network monsters. Social networking began to grow about the time we were launching our management company. I was an early adopter of blogging, Twitter and Facebook. Learning the art of building massive followings was an interesting challenge I took on with fervor. At the time, there was a service called Twitter Grader where one could see stats and one's ranking as an influential Twitterer in their city, state, country and the world. I quickly became obsessed with becoming the number one Twitterer in my area. The Nashville area is full of celebrities and influencers making my quest quite the challenge. I was so obsessed with becoming number one in Brentwood, Tennessee, I reached out to the top five

creating MONSTERS

ranking Twitterers to connect and size up my competition. I found the top four fairly easy to pass up, but there was a very savvy marketer holding down the number one position. The number one Twitterer had been using Twitter a year prior to my start, making him difficult to pass. I eventually claimed the number one spot and held on to it until Twitter Grader ceased to exist. Ironically, my nephew interviewed for a job at the former number one Twitterer's marketing firm. During the interview, the man made the statement to my nephew: "Your uncle sure is obsessed with being number one!" Although I am embarrassed to admit it, those words confirmed that I had become a social network monster.

When I pitch artists to record labels, one of the first things most label A&R reps do is check out the artist's Twitter and Facebook accounts to determine their "social net worth." At times, an artist's "social net worth" seems more important than the music they create. The crazy thing is anyone can build a facade following through a number of different methods. Someone can have ten thousand Twitter followers—none of whom ever see or care about their Tweets, thanks to follower-building software. It really takes hit radio songs and heavy touring to build a genuine large following, and that normally takes place after an artist is signed to a record label. Sure, there will be a few who go viral on the Internet without radio and touring, but those are anomalies. Unfortunately, the priority placed on the number of followers encourages new artists to become social network monsters.

While social networking is fun, it can quickly usher in a dark element. Many users post things to draw attention to themselves so they appear to be living the dream. If an artist focuses too much on what other artists post, the artist can experience feelings of depression and jealousy. I don't think God intends for us to live in such a dark place. My advice to anyone is to keep things in check. Use social networks as a tool to engage those who are interested in one's music and ministry, but don't allow the obsession of getting more followers to overtake one's daily life in an attempt to increase self-worth.

SOCIAL NETWORK MONSTERS

A word of caution should also be said regarding spending too much time reading what others are posting. While I do recommend supporting others with retweets and shares, it's easy to become obsessed with comparing oneself to others and allowing envy to creep in. Envy for what others are doing is food for the monster.

It's also important to remember that social networking creates a permanent record on the Internet of what we post. I can personally say there are a few Twitter rants I posted over the years I wish would disappear. Frustration with airlines, hotels and restaurants have presented a weak spot for me. When I'm wronged, why not turn to Twitter and broadcast it to the world? Unfortunately, one can now be sued for such comments as they have the potential to hurt the reputation of a person or business. Moreover, most Twitter rants normally don't reflect the love of Jesus, which presents an even bigger issue for Christians. Celebrities, artists and other public figures have influence over their followers and can taint someone's reputation quickly. Recently, a top Christian artist with a massive Twitter following had a bad experience with an airline and quickly turned to Twitter to let the world know about it. The rant about the airlines reminded me of similar rants I have posted. A lawsuit was filed against the artist by an airline employee. I'm sure the artist now regrets the Tweet, as the lawsuit was broadcast across local media. Someone who makes a living singing about Jesus now has their negative rant permanently on the Internet. That particular artist has done a lot of good toward spreading the Gospel, and it would be a shame for one little incident of human error to overshadow the goodness. Thankfully, God uses my wife, Diana, to remind me to be kind when I am wronged and feel the need to Tweet. God tells us, in the book of James, slander isn't such a good practice.

> *Humble yourselves before the Lord, and he will exalt you.*
> *Do not speak evil against one another, brothers. The one who speaks against a brother or judges his brother, speaks evil against the*

> *law and judges the law. But if you judge the law, you are*
> *not a doer of the law but a judge.*
> (James 4:10-11, ESV)

I have a sneaky suspicion James 4:10-11 applies to what we say about hotels, airlines and restaurants who don't give us good service.

Just as ill will can be spread through social networks, the love of God can also be spread. I'm often encouraged by those who post regular positive messages. A good friend of mine posts the most encouraging things on Facebook. Every morning, I know I will wake up to an encouraging word from Dusty on Facebook. I'm sure he encounters not so great days just like the rest of the world, but his consistent positive encouragement on Facebook gives thousands of followers hope and perspective.

One artist we work with also balances social networking especially well. The artist gives followers insight into their daily life. At times, the posts expose vulnerability regarding things the artist is struggling with, and at other times, the artist offers encouraging words. When the artist posts Scripture, it appears heartfelt and many pay attention.

Social networking has glorified the word "following." The core of the word "following" feels a bit disturbing to me when used to describe anyone who subscribes to my Twitter feed. "Following" has historically been associated with religious and cult leaders. Jesus, John the Baptist, Paul, Gandhi, Muhammed, Joseph Smith, Jim Jones (remember him?) and David Koresh all had or still have followers. The word "follower" normally describes someone's dedicated belief in an individual or an individual's set of beliefs. I think, at times, social network celebrities begin to feel like religious leaders as their following grows. The power of getting others to act on things one posts is exhilarating! I know my ego explodes with joy when others retweet or share my posts. Did I just say my EGO (as in "Easing God Out") explodes with joy when someone retweets me? I am so thankful my God is forgiving, as the joy in Him is so much greater than the false and temporal joy created by ego and any social network.

Putting accountability in place is a good idea for anyone who uses social networks. Having a trusted person who lets one know when one's social network actions appear unhealthy will help users avoid much grief. When any sign of the social network monster creeps in, knowing God is bigger should help us stuff the monster in the closet and refuse to feed it.

chapter fourteen:
THE ABOMINABLE SNOWMAN

Most of us have read the story in Genesis. Adam and Eve give into temptation by taking a bite of the apple, and the snowball of sin in the world begins to roll.

We are all faced with temptation on a regular basis. What we do with temptation determines our path in life. The temptation of doing something to become popular or famous is one of the most effective and dangerous tools the enemy uses. As an artist manager, I try to help artists anticipate and recognize temptation early on. If they learn to avoid temptation, their careers will bear much fruit; but the pursuit of fame will most certainly yield a harvest of rotten fruit. Jesus was very frank about the dangers of temptation.

> *Woe to the world for temptations to sin! For it is necessary that temptations come, but woe to the one by whom the temptation comes! And if your hand or your foot causes you to sin, cut it off and throw it away. It is better for you to enter life crippled or lame than with two hands or two feet to be thrown into the eternal fire.*

> *And if your eye causes you to sin, tear it out and throw it away.*
> *It is better for you to enter life with one eye than with two eyes*
> *to be thrown into the hell of fire.*
> (Matthew 18:7-9, ESV)

Jesus Himself experienced temptation from Satan while He was in the wilderness to fast and pray. Knowing the power and danger of temptation, Jesus made praying for deliverance from temptation a key element in His instructions on how we should pray.

> *And lead us not into temptation, but deliver us from evil.*
> (Matthew 6:13, ESV)

One artist we worked with wanted to be famous so badly that they were willing to do just about anything for fame. While the artist was in the studio working on a Christian record, they were having a difficult time hitting notes and capturing a great vocal pass. There was a deadline approaching to finish the record, and the artist was feeling pressured. A young producer convinced the artist to drink whiskey in order to sing the notes. This particular artist had never drunk alcohol and had made a decision earlier in life not to drink. The young producer knew about those convictions, yet still encouraged the action. I am certainly not the alcohol police, as the Bible tells me that Jesus turned water into the finest wine; but there is importance in standing strong in your convictions whatever they may be. God puts those convictions in place for a reason. I was saddened and disturbed by how quickly the artist set his convictions aside in order to do whatever it takes to "make it." Diana and I had spent hours preparing this artist for these very scenarios he would encounter in the industry and encouraged him to prepare an escape plan for those situations. Sadly, temptation and pressure from the producer trumped any escape plan he may have laid out in advance.

Assuming my role of mentor and protector, I confronted the young producer and tried to help him understand how detrimental his actions could be for the young artist's life and career. He had created the perfect catalyst for addiction: "Drink this and you will sing well." I've been around enough addiction in my life to recognize the time bomb. If the alcohol trick works, the artist could quickly become dependent on the crutch every time they sing. What about alternatives like tea with lemon and honey or recording the song in a key more comfortable for the artist's voice? The young producer was offended when I confronted him with the issue, and the artist sided with the producer. Not only did the artist carelessly set his convictions aside, but he embraced the violator and was angry at me for looking out for his convictions. What a perfect meal the enemy cooked up to feed the monster. Unfortunately, the incident drove a wedge in the relationship between me and the artist.

When the artist's first single didn't perform well at radio, the artist was devastated. While I was disappointed with the lack of radio success, I wasn't surprised. Is God really going to fully bless a Christian song recorded under those conditions? While I don't have God's answer to that question, it is one to ponder. The artist's bad decision shouldn't have been surprising as I recall an earlier conversation with his parents about their son becoming a sex symbol, and their exact words were "whatever it takes." The "whatever it takes to be successful" attitude was used often by the artist's parents. Unfortunately, "whatever it takes" mixed with "alcohol" and "sex symbol" creates the perfect cocktail for disaster. Billy Ray Cyrus, the father of Miley Cyrus, might have some words of wisdom regarding the "whatever it takes" approach. I can only pray God will cause the advice we shared to linger in the artist's mind and give him something to draw from when encountering future temptations.

When an artist gives into the celebrity temptation, the snowball effect takes place. It's like pouring Miracle Grow on the monster gene. The snowball gains momentum and becomes so big it morphs into the abominable snowman. The abominable snowman listens to no one and convinces themselves they are the biggest and baddest while daring anyone to challenge them. I've seen a few of those monsters walking around, and honestly, no one wants to be around them.

When I see a successful Christian headliner refuse to allow the opening artist access to the full stage and lights, it's a sure sign that the monster is present. The God I serve calls us to serve one another.

> *The greatest among you shall be your servant. Whoever exalts himself will be humbled, and whoever humbles himself will be exalted.*
> (Matthew 23:11-12, ESV)

When I read Matthew 23 I don't see any mentions of exceptions for celebrity Christian artists. Yes, denying opening artists access to full production is a normal practice in mainstream music, but doesn't God call believers to be different? What if denying the opening act full access to sound and lights prevented one person from being impacted enough to find Jesus? Obviously, the headliner has worked hard to earn that status on the music success pyramid, but does that exalt them in the eyes of God or earn them special privileges? Jesus had some powerful words for two of His disciples who thought they were pretty special.

> *And James and John, the sons of Zebedee, came up to him and said to him, "Teacher, we want you to do for us whatever we ask of you." And he said to them, "What do you want me to do for you?" And they said to him, "Grant us to sit, one at your right hand and one at your left, in your glory." Jesus said to them, "You do not know what you are asking. Are you able to drink the cup that I drink, or to be baptized with the baptism with which I am baptized?" And they said to him, "We are able." And Jesus said to them, "The cup that I drink you will drink, and with the baptism with which I am baptized, you will be*

baptized, but to sit at my right hand or at my left is not mine to grant, but it is for those for whom it has been prepared."
(Mark 10:35-40, ESV)

Shining above some of the disappointing examples, there are some Christian headliners who manage the monster well and model great examples for others. TobyMac is one I have witnessed in action. His incredibly successful music career could very well have created the biggest monster of all. Instead, he goes out of his way to make other artists feel equal. Unlike some headliners, Toby allows opening artists access to all parts of his stage. It's apparent Toby understands the production he travels with is owned by God, and he treats it as such. He serves as a great mentor for young artists. I have worked with several of Toby's band members, and they are all stand-up Jesus followers. Toby has taken great care in surrounding himself with a godly team in an effort to foster a monster-free environment. MercyMe is another act I've seen show extreme kindness to new artists. While I haven't had the opportunity to work around Casting Crowns, their reputation of kindness and humility reverberates throughout the industry.

God knew, without Him in our lives, we would find it difficult to resist being tempted by desires for pleasure, fame and other things that being a celebrity promises. Jesus tells us:

Do not love the world or the things in the world. If anyone loves the world, the love of the Father is not in him. For all that is in the world—the desires of the flesh and the desires of the eyes and pride of life—is not from the Father but is from the world.
(1 John 2:15-16, ESV)

He is calling Christians to live differently from those of the world. Through Jesus, we can find the power to resist worldly desires that feed the

creating MONSTERS

monster. Walking in God's light will melt the snow, making it impossible for the abominable snowman to exist.

chapter fifteen:
MONSTERS OF FINANCE

Financial responsibility is an area where I see a large number of artists struggle. I guess it shouldn't be a surprise as the struggle is rampant throughout society, even with non-artists. Unfortunately, most receive little to no financial training in the early school years. I remember hearing sermons on tithing during my adolescent years, but I don't recall one sermon on managing finances with excellence. Thankfully, Dave Ramsey showed up on the scene to offer some wise teaching on finances. I really wish Dave would launch a program specifically designed for artists. For some unknown reason, many artists eschew financial responsibility in the name of art. Some believe their art gives them a free pass to use other people's money along their journey to success with no obligation to repay their financial debt. Many creatives are focused on the dream of their art exploding in popularity and an abundance of wealth. During the process, they fail to recognize those who invest in their career. Surprisingly, this attitude is quite rampant in Christian music.

When we launched our artist management company, I would have never guessed some of the financial craziness we would encounter from artists flying the Christian banner. Most newbie artists are filled with fear of the "evil" record labels and managers due to the many stories circulated by other artists who were taken advantage of in some way. My experience has been quite the opposite and has proven to show many of the artists are the ones to be feared.

We signed one of our first artists with such excitement—artist and manager on a journey of Christian music bliss! As the first few commission checks rolled in, we were thankful because we had been living on savings through the early launch of our management company. We were finally seeing the possibility of making a living as artist managers. Just as quickly as the first commission checks began to arrive, they ceased showing up in the mailbox. The artist was playing shows but somehow found a way to justify not paying us our commission for the shows. They apparently had bills to pay and made the decision to use our commission to pay them. Our work on their behalf was easily dismissed in their thought process. Maybe the artist received a word from God giving them exemption from paying those working for them? If so, I apparently missed God's voice on my end. I tried to help them understand that our commission was not their money to play with, and their actions could easily be viewed as embezzlement. While embezzlement may sound like a harsh word to use, it perfectly describes how it feels to be on the non-receiving side of a commission commitment. I often ask artists the question, "What if you showed up to a church, played a show, and afterwards the pastor of the church decided to pay his mortgage with the money they had committed to you?"

Shortly thereafter, we began working with another artist, and we secured a songwriting placement for him on a compilation record guaranteed to sell a minimum of seventy-five thousand units. We agreed to begin working on his behalf while we were still working through the official formalities of the contract. Down south, that's known as a "gentlemen's agreement." God's Word calls it "honoring your promise." Unfortunately for us, the artist viewed things in a much different light. He informed us he was exempt from compensating us for the song placement since our contract hadn't actually been signed. A pass from God, I'm guessing?

Another Christian artist we worked with bought T-shirts from a vendor with whom we connected him. The artist sold the shirts, stiffed the vendor and even became irritated when the vendor would call looking for their money. I found the situation tough to understand as the non-believing T-shirt vendor actually asked me, "Is that how Christians operate?" How in the world could anyone ever have a conversation with this vendor about Jesus after that experience?

While I understand anyone can encounter difficult financial times, I don't think God calls us to walk away from debt and never look back. Those actions are an absolute mockery of how God tells us to handle debt. Had I been that artist, I would have set up some kind of payment plan, offered to mow the vendor's lawn or offered some other way of sweat equity to make good on my debt. Walking away from debt is not an accepted practice taught in the Bible, and it is one of the lamest non-Christian things an artist can do on their journey of representing Jesus.

In speaking with other artist managers over the years, I have come to realize my experiences aren't unique. You would be surprised if I listed the well-known Christian artists and worship leaders who have stiffed their managers or others. Why do so many Christian artists feel exempt from God's instruction on honoring financial commitments? The Bible gives us undeniable instruction on paying what is owed.

> *Therefore one must be in subjection, not only to avoid God's wrath but also for the sake of conscience. For because of this you also pay taxes, for the authorities are ministers of God, attending to this very thing. Pay to all what is owed to them: taxes to whom taxes are owed, revenue to whom*

> *revenue is owed, respect to whom respect is owed,*
> *honor to whom honor is owed.*
> (Romans 13:5-7, ESV)

In Psalms, we are given a fairly direct description of someone who borrows and doesn't pay back.

> *The wicked borrows but does not pay back,*
> *but the righteous is generous and gives.*
> (Psalm 37:21, ESV)

For myself, I never wish to be lumped in with the wicked. Paying debts and honoring commitments have always been huge priorities. A real tension arose as we noticed the careless abandonment that some artists have toward paying what is owed. More than just concern over me being paid is worry over where their hearts are for following God's instruction on finances and paying debt. As believers, when we make commitments, we are making a promise before God and representing Him to others. God gives us instruction in Ecclesiastes in regards to making vows.

> *When you vow a vow to God, do not delay paying it, for he has no*
> *pleasure in fools. Pay what you vow. It is better that you should not*
> *vow than that you should vow and not pay. Let not your mouth lead*
> *you into sin, and do not say before the messenger that it was a mistake.*
> *Why should God be angry at your voice and destroy the work of your*
> *hands? For when dreams increase and words grow many, there is*
> *vanity; but God is the one you must fear.*
> (Ecclesiastes 5:4-7, ESV)

So how do we deal with financial monsters? Just like the other monsters we have discussed, if we don't feed them, they can't survive. Over the years, I have become pretty savvy at recognizing early signs of the financial monster. Exposing the signs, praying for the artists and mentoring is what God calls us to do. It can be unpopular with artists at times, but I refuse to ignore poor financial responsibility. Many attempt to play the "I'm a poor, struggling missionary just spreading God's Word" card. In the past, I have allowed those words to play with my emotions, and therefore, let poor financial responsibility slide. Now, I address it firmly with any early signs of poor financial responsibility. Finances and commitment are apparently important to God as He addresses both quite frequently throughout the Bible. God can and will give artists the ability to starve the financial monster.

chapter sixteen:
MONSTERS OF COMMITMENT

Growing up in a God-centered family afforded me great teaching through the example my parents lived. One of my biggest takeaways from childhood was learning the meaning of integrity. Dad taught me that aside from following God, integrity is a person's biggest asset. Integrity is also apparently a big deal to God as there is quite a bit of real estate dedicated to it in the Bible. A few verses that I keep close by to remind me of the importance of integrity include:

> *But you have upheld me because of my integrity,*
> *and set me in your presence forever.*
> (Psalm 41:12, ESV)

> *The integrity of the upright guides them, but the crookedness*
> *of the treacherous destroys them.*
> (Proverbs 11:3, ESV)

> *The righteous who walks in his integrity—blessed*
> *are his children after him!*
> (Proverbs 20:7, ESV)

When I see a person exuding integrity, I can usually trace it back to their parents. Even many I worked with in the mainstream music industry hold integrity with high regard. Commitment plays an important role in most business relationships, and it exposes one's level of integrity to the world. During my years of working at both mainstream and Christian record companies, I generally experienced a high level of integrity. Of course, there are normally contracts in place to help folks keep their integrity in tact, but there is also a high level of respect and pride in honoring commitments.

Surprisingly, when I entered artist management I began to experience something a bit different. First of all, I noticed many artists were leery of making commitments as their minds had been filled with horror stories of bad deals and contracts. While I have heard many of the same stories, I also understand that the music business has evolved and much of the "music business swindling artists out of money" of the past has been forced out. Technology has made much of the business that was once hidden very transparent. In the past, artists with large platforms who felt mistreated used their voice to broadcast to the world how they were wronged. Their voices were often heard louder than those they accused as most business entities quietly default to litigation to settle disputes. While I understand an artist's hesitancy to enter into a contract, they certainly have an opportunity to carry out due diligence when considering partnering with a business. In Christian music, I would hope that process includes prayer. Prayer and due diligence should help make a wise decision as the Christian music business is quite small.

As we launched our artist management company, we expected a high level of integrity from artists. After all, we would be working with Christians right? We were advised by trusted veterans in the business to use contracts.

MONSTERS OF COMMITMENT

While we followed the advice, we were also willing to begin working with artists before contracts were finalized. Big mistake! We had several experiences where we worked for artists for a year, only to find them avoiding making the commitment official. When it came time to pay us, they would lean on the fact that a contract hadn't been signed. As a result, contracts became a much bigger priority for us. However, thinking contracts would solve commitment issues was our second biggest mistake.

One of the artists we worked with joyously allowed us to help build their platform. After years of hard work developing them as an artist and songwriter, we secured them a record label. The day they signed the record deal, something in their demeanor changed. Diana picked up on it immediately, while I was a little slower to recognize the change; and I probably chose to ignore it. The day following the record deal signing, the artist hit us with "here's why we don't think we should pay you commission on a large part of our advance." I was extremely shocked and disappointed that the thought of not paying us would even enter their mind. We had invested a great deal of our lives over a few years making little to no money while preparing them to get a record deal, and this was how they were saying thank you? It was their parent who delivered the message, making the artist's trail to the absence of integrity obvious. Eventually, the same artist would walk away from our contract as if it never existed, once again being encouraged to do so by parents who proudly wave the Christian banner. Was this really happening in the Christian music industry? I pray the artist eventually realizes the mistake they made in taking their parents' poor advice and being dishonorable. Hearing stories from other managers, I've realized we weren't the first or only ones to experience an absence of integrity from artists in Christian music. While there are plenty of artists who operate with a high level of integrity, it's sad to see even one Christian who doesn't.

Clearly, the monster desires to control our commitments. Stripping integrity and honor from a believer is a crafty way the monster prevents one from reaching God's purpose for their life and ministry. Should we expect a non-believer to be receptive to a message from someone with a reputation of not honoring commitments? As I stated earlier, even many operating in the mainstream music industry regard integrity with a high level of importance. As believers, shouldn't we desire to show the world how to live with integrity? Honoring commitments is one of the most visible opportunities we have to do so. God can give us the power to resist the monster.

chapter seventeen:
MONSTER MUSIC

    Music is an incredibly powerful force. Amazingly, it helps us through both good and bad times in life. I've experienced music's power in some of life's most joyous celebrations, and yet, music has also helped me process some of the darkest times in life. Contrary to what some may believe, I think God uses both Christian and mainstream music to stir and change human emotion. God may have actually used some of those secular records my youth leader encouraged me to burn to help me on my journey to finding Him. On the other hand, Satan recognizes the power in music, too, so it's very likely he used music as well to make my journey to finding God a little more difficult.

    One of the most well-known mentions of music in the Bible was when David was summoned to play his harp to soothe King Saul's troubled soul. In an interesting twist, God brings torment to Saul's soul but then uses David's harp playing to assuage the torment.

Now the Spirit of the Lord departed from Saul, and a harmful spirit from the Lord tormented him. And Saul's servants said to him,

"Behold now, a harmful spirit from God is tormenting you. Let our lord now command your servants who are before you to seek out a man who is skillful in playing the lyre, and when the harmful spirit from God is upon you, he will play it, and you will be well." So Saul said to his servants, "Provide for me a man who can play well and bring him to me." One of the young men answered, "Behold, I have seen a son of Jesse the Bethlehemite, who is skillful in playing, a man of valor, a man of war, prudent in speech, and a man of good presence, and the Lord is with him." Therefore Saul sent messengers to Jesse and said, "Send me David your son, who is with the sheep." And Jesse took a donkey laden with bread and a skin of wine and a young goat and sent them by David his son to Saul. And David came to Saul and entered his service. And Saul loved him greatly, and he became his armor-bearer. And Saul sent to Jesse, saying, "Let David remain in my service, for he has found favor in my sight." And whenever the harmful spirit from God was upon Saul, David took the lyre and played it with his hand. So Saul was refreshed and was well, and the harmful spirit departed from him.
(1 Samuel 16:14-23, ESV)

God also used music to give Elisha powerful words to speak.

And Elisha said, "As the Lord of hosts lives, before whom I stand, were it not that I have regard for Jehoshaphat the king of Judah, I would neither look at you nor see you. But now bring me a musician." And when the musician played, the hand of the Lord c ame upon him. And he said, "Thus says the Lord, 'I will make this dry streambed full of pools.'
(2 Kings 3:14-16, ESV)

While music plays a significant role throughout the Bible, those two examples show God using music for specific purposes. Clearly, the ability to create music is a powerful tool He gifts to some. Even when artists with rock star attitudes and lifestyles make it to the top of the Christian radio charts, God can still use the music to draw the lost to Jesus. A good friend of mine, Pete Orta, has an incredible story of how God used his music before he was actually saved. Pete was a member of the Christian rock group Petra. He played for large audiences around the world impacting thousands of lives. Pete didn't have a relationship with Jesus during that time, but God still used him to spread the Gospel through music. Thankfully, Pete eventually found Jesus and is now being used by God in huge kingdom-building ways. A few years back, Pete founded In Triumph, a ministry that rescues and disciples troubled young men.

While God can and will use music made by non-believers for His purposes, it doesn't mean the non-believers He uses will spend eternity with Him in heaven. Pete's story of redemption is glorious, but sadly, not all will end in a similar way. The Bible tells us in Luke 12:48 that God expects much from those who are given much. Clearly, large platforms fall on the side of much. If Luke 12 is indeed true, then celebrity status comes with giant responsibility and eternal ramifications. I can't imagine standing before God after living the monster-controlled life of a rock star and answering His question, "So, how did you use the platform I gave you?"

chapter eighteen:
KILLING THE MONSTER

So we know the monster lives. Now what? A well-fed monster can gain enormous influence over the person it dwells within—an influence so strong that outside voices of reason, and even the voice of God, can often go unheard. Feeling responsible for feeding and creating the monster, we become determined to find a way to break through. We must find a way to kill the monster!

I have found the task of dismantling the monster an extremely difficult and seemingly impossible undertaking. As egos grow, the monster raises a massive defense shield to protect his or her ego from outside intruders. The defense shield repels even the closest friends and loved ones as it perceives them as enemies. The monster surrounds itself with "yes" men and women who are plentiful and standing in line just to get the opportunity to hang out with the monster. Monsters like to hang out with other monsters, and anyone who speaks truth and wisdom quickly becomes the enemy.

When I married my wife over a decade ago, I entered into a celebrity family. My step-daughter is a multi-Platinum selling, GRAMMY®- nominated artist who was mentored by some of the best Dr. Frankensteins in the music industry. She found herself worshipped by millions of fans at a very young age. In her case, becoming a celebrity at fifteen years old wasn't planned. She simply wanted to sing. I think it's impossible for anyone under twenty-five to even begin to comprehend the implications of becoming famous. A quick look at the lives of most childhood stars shows the negative effects being worshipped often leaves behind. Their adult life is filled with trouble as they attempt to fill the emptiness the childhood stardom leaves within them. None of us were designed by God to be worshipped, so it would be ridiculous to expect a young person to walk through a celebrity experience perfectly unscathed.

Watching my step-daughter struggle with an ego that was planted and fertilized by the music industry helped me understand some of the difficulty artists encounter. Thankfully, Diana was by her side to help protect her from some of the craziness. Even so, the struggle to maturity was enormous. When one is surrounded by people willing to attend to one's every need, basic survival skills become skewed. As with any human, if someone serves our every need, then it's impossible to realize our true dependence on God. What happens when the "yes" people disappear? Complete emptiness is inevitable. In the case of my step-daughter, she was abandoned by many of her "yes" people the minute she encountered a difficult time in her life. Many in the Christian music industry abandoned and shunned her at a time when she needed their love the most. Thankfully, she had a mom and grandmother who cared for her way beyond any success she had achieved. Many prayers were lifted to God on her behalf; and as He promises, God was there to fill her emptiness. I can't imagine what it's like for a childhood celebrity who doesn't know God or who doesn't have friends and family who lead them in His direction and intercede with prayer. Interestingly, today if you asked Diana if she could travel back in time, would she have allowed her fifteen-year-old daughter to enter the music industry at such a young age, her reply would be a resounding "no."

God gives us great examples in nature. One of the greatest is watching a mother bird with her babies. She feeds them and attends their every need while they are younglings. Once they begin to show signs of strength, she pushes them out of the nest in order to teach them to fly, which is similar to our role as artist managers. I not only want to see artists fly, I want to see see them fly with the integrity and the purpose God created them for. There is nothing more rewarding than seeing an artist live their lives according to God's plan.

My struggle with helping artists build platforms is similar to that of parenting. No matter how intentional we are with mentoring, it is impossible to control the outcome. I'm often reminded of the old saying, "You can buy them books and send them to school, but you can't make them learn." As much as I would like to tame every monster I encounter, the only one I can directly control is the one that desires to reside in me. Maybe my personal experience in battling the flesh can be used to help artists realize and understand the existence of the monster that fights to control their minds and actions. While it may be a daunting task, it's one I feel called by God to take on. Exposing the monster early on and encouraging artists to allow God's Word to be their manual for living life will significantly impact the monster survival rate. After all, God is the ultimate monster slayer.

chapter nineteen:
TURN ON THE LIGHTS

As a child, I remember having a fear that a monster lived under my bed or in my bedroom closet. My dad had a solution for squelching my fear, and it proved to work brilliantly every time. Dad would simply turn on the lights and have me look under the bed and in the closet to show me nothing was there.

Walking through life, I sometimes fear the scariest monster of all resides in me. So what do I do with the fear? Using the technique I learned from my dad, I simply turn on the lights. The quickest way I know to turn the lights on is to diligently study God's Word, spend time in prayer with Him and surround myself with true Jesus followers who hold me accountable. With the lights turned on, God will certainly reveal any sign of a monster. As long as the lights are on, there is no way for the monster to control my mind or actions; but the minute I allow the lights to dim, the monster will begin to surface.

For me, turning the lights on often reveals Dr. Frankenstein at work. While I feel called to work as an artist manager, I struggle with how to walk

creating MONSTERS

out the manager role without creating monsters. Despite my best efforts, some monster-driven hearts have slipped through on my watch. Even though it seems like those were mistakes on my part, I can't help but think God put me in those artists' lives for a reason. If only for a short season, God can use us to mentor them. While it may be frustrating to see an artist feeding the monster, I continually remind myself that my role is to plant seeds and lead them to the light switch. God is the only one who can illuminate, and ultimately defeat, the monster.

MY PRAYER

God, thank You for loving me and calling me into the role You designed specifically for me. I pray You would give me wisdom as I help manage the ministries and careers of artists You have called for Your purpose. Please help us recognize the monsters present in our flesh as a result of the fall. We ask for Your help. Thank You for giving us a way to overcome the monsters. I pray You would use us to help spread the news of Your son, Jesus, as He is the only one we are called to make famous. Please kill the monsters in all of us and let Your glory shine!

Do not be deceived: God is not mocked, for whatever one sows, that will he also reap. For the one who sows to his own flesh will from the flesh reap corruption, but the one who sows to the Spirit will from the Spirit reap eternal life.
(Galatians 6:7-8, ESV)

FOR YOUR FREE

creating MONSTERS study guide

VISIT

www.keithstancil.com

about the author

Keith Stancil is the President/CEO of Artist Garden Entertainment, an artist management and marketing firm based in Brentwood, Tennessee. Keith served twenty years in various sales and marketing roles at Capitol/EMI, Warner/Elektra/Atlantic and Word Entertainment. His most recent label years were served in the role of Vice President of General Markets/International/Digital for Word Entertainment. While personally overseeing sales of over fourteen million records, Keith worked on sales and marketing strategies for Garth Brooks, Tim McGraw, Tina Turner, Madonna, Metallica, Red Hot Chili Peppers, MercyMe, Amy Grant, Faith Hill, Jaci Velasquez, Hillsong, Randy Travis, Point of Grace, Francesca Battistelli, the WOW Brand and many others.

Keith and his wife, Diana, launched Artist Garden Entertainment in 2009. In addition to artist management, Keith serves as a marketing consultant on projects with various independent artists and record labels spanning contemporary Christian music and Christian hip-hop with a client list that includes Reach Records, RMG Music, Save The City Records, Lampmode Recordings, Collision Records, Flame and Social Club.

In 2009, Keith founded TheMusicGardener.com blog which was honored multiple years by the *Nashville Scene* in the "Best of Nashville" awards. He regularly blogs about music industry trends, artist development, music marketing and new music.

Keith is the founder of *Finding Fame In Jesus' Name University*, a school designed to equip those pursuing careers on platforms that offer the potential for fame.

In addition to Keith's personal ventures, he also serves on the board for *In Triumph*, a non-profit ministry for young men.

connect with keith

Keith would love to connect and hear thoughts or ideas you may have after reading Creating Monsters.

WEBSITES

keithstancil.com
themusicgardener.com
artistgardenentertainment.com

SOCIALS

Facebook - http://www.facebook.com/authorkeithstancil
Twitter - https://twitter.com/keithstancil
Pinterest - http://pinterest.com/keithstancil

BOOKING

Keith would love to speak at your event or host a mini *Finding Fame In Jesus' Name University* workshop.
To book Keith please e-mail: keithstancil@gmail.com

Finding Fame in Jesus' Name University

FFJN University is a school designed to go a little deeper into the ideas explored in Creating Monsters. Our objective is to equip those working in or pursuing careers that involve platforms and potential fame, with tools to assist them on their journey of making Jesus famous. Artists, musicians, actors, athletes, speakers and corporate ladder climbers are all invited to join us.

Apply To Attend FFJN University

If you are interested in attending FFJN University, please visit **keithstancil.com**

IN TRIUMPH MINISTRIES

AFTERCARE YOUTH

Due to the influx and massive amounts of teens aging out of the foster care system with disorders and addictions throughout the U.S., it has seemed almost impossible for the church or state to respond to such a colossal area of need. This burden resulted in allowing us to partake in shouldering this responsibility, while providing a biblical solution. As secular institutions continue to treat humanity's fallen nature with psychiatric medications and therapy, we have come to fully understand that the "root" of the problem is depravity. And unlike any other diagnoses, when total depravity is recognized, and a person truly repents, a total transformation is possible.

ADDICTED YOUNG ADULTS

It is difficult to consider, though at times necessary, institutionalizing every drug addicted youth as an answer for correcting their habitual and external behaviors. As many times as "success rates" are implied, one cannot negate the evidence of the "relapse rates" within our secular facilities. Unfortunately, some institutions have become a "bad seed" by capitalizing on financial gain rather than an individual's restoration, and thus offering only provisional answers instead of productive ones.

OUR RESPONSE

The evolution of self-centeredness can be identified in today's self-esteem, self-help, or any other varieties that the self-improvement industry is selling. One does not have to be a Greek Philosopher or a Ph.D to understand that nothing changes until something outside of itself interferes. With that being said, the search for deity is paramount if our depravity is to be transformed. Therefore, without a God who interferes, humanity is left with the insanity of repackaging self and expecting a different result. Consequently, we are, until He is.

In Triumph brings a systematic approach to the Gospel, and gives time to those in need to learn how to make it applicable. We preach Christ and disciple so that young men will know how to navigate as Biblical husbands, fathers, and captains of their ship. So as we do provide food, clothes and shelter for the "least of these," our primary focus is providing the framework where a genuine commitment to Christ can be fostered.

Made in the USA
Charleston, SC
11 November 2015